812
Hit

Hit t̲ ... and
other new voices of
the American
theater.

X

| DATE | | | |
|---|---|---|---|
| OCT 10 '97 | | | |
| NOV 2 '98 | | | |
| NOV 18 '98 | | | |
| | | | |
| | | | |
| | | | |
| | | | |
| | | | |
| | | | |
| | | | |
| | | | |

Chatham Public Library
Chatham, NY 12037

BAKER & TAYLOR

# HIT THE NERVE

Here are some other Edge Books
from Henry Holt you will enjoy:

*A Way Out of No Way*
*Writings About Growing Up Black in America*
edited by Jacqueline Woodson

*American Eyes*
*New Asian-American Short Stories*
*for Young Adults*
edited by Lori M. Carlson

*Barrio Streets Carnival Dreams*
*Three Generations of Latino Artistry*
edited by Lori M. Carlson

*The Beautiful Days of My Youth*
*My Six Months in Auschwitz and Plaszow*
by Ana Novac
translated from the French by George L. Newman

*Cool Salsa*
*Bilingual Poems on Growing Up Latino*
*in the United States*
edited by Lori M. Carlson

*Damned Strong Love*
*The True Story of Willi G. and Stefan K.*
by Lutz van Dijk
translated from the German by Elizabeth D. Crawford

*The Long Season of Rain*
by Helen Kim

*One Bird*
by Kyoko Mori

*Over the Water*
by Maude Casey

*The Rebellious Alphabet*
by Jorge Diaz
translated from the Spanish by Geoffrey Fox

*The Roller Birds of Rampur*
by Indi Rana

*Shizuko's Daughter*
by Kyoko Mori

*Song of Be*
by Lesley Beake

*Spyglass*
*An Autobiography*
by Hélène Deschamps

*We Are Witnesses*
*The Diaries of Five Teenagers Who Died*
*in the Holocaust*
by Jacob Boas

NEW VOICES
■ OF THE ■
AMERICAN
THEATER

EDITED BY
STEPHEN
VINCENT
BRENNAN

HENRY HOLT AND COMPANY ■ NEW YORK

Henry Holt and Company, Inc.
*Publishers since 1866*
115 West 18th Street
New York, New York 10011

Henry Holt is a registered
trademark of Henry Holt and Company, Inc.

Compilation and introduction copyright © 1997
by Stephen Vincent Brennan
All rights reserved.
Published in Canada by Fitzhenry & Whiteside Ltd.,
195 Allstate Parkway, Markham, Ontario L3R 4T8.

Library of Congress Cataloging-in-Publication Data
Hit the nerve: new voices of the American theater /
    edited by Stephen Vincent Brennan.
        p.    cm.
1. American drama—20th century.
I. Brennan, Stephen Vincent.
PS634.H58    1996    812'.5408—dc21    96-49532

ISBN 0-8050-4817-0

First Edition—1997

Printed in the United States of America
on acid-free paper. ∞

10  9  8  7  6  5  4  3  2  1

# Acknowledgments

Many people helped in assembling this anthology. I wish to particularly thank Judy Boals of Berman, Boals & Flynn; Andrea Chapin of the *New Theater Review;* Brian Murphy of Frankfort, Garbus, Klein & Selz; Matt Lewis of the William Morris Agency; Ron Hussey of Simon & Schuster; Carol Christiansen of Bantam Doubleday Dell; Sarah Jane Leigh of International Creative Management; and Frank Rich, for advice and assistance, in many cases, well beyond the call.

I also wish to thank my editor, Marc Aronson, and his associate, Matthew Rosen, for their always thoughtful and always generous help with this book.

Chatham Public Library
Chatham, NY 12037
C.1

Chatham Public Library
Chatham, NY 12037

For Jenny, with all my heart

# Contents

# HIT THE NERVE

# Introduction

BY STEPHEN VINCENT BRENNAN

I watched spellbound. The man with a knife roared and lunged at his friend, who over and over again, ducked the blade and spun out, shouting, spitting, hissing; egging-on his assailant. The other men on stage moved to stop or block or separate them. Someone was going to be killed. I was sure of it. Things had gone too far. It felt as though something dangerous was loose in the room. Suddenly the knife began to thrust upward, as if aimed at God, and a dam-burst of rage and pain geysered out and became a kind of angry, despairing prayer. In that moment I became that man onstage. My eyes stung. In that moment I hated God and wished to cut him, too. We all did. Our bright wet eyes shone like lanterns in the darkened theater.

This was several years ago. The play was August Wilson's *Ma Rainey's Black Bottom,* performed at the Yale Repertory Theater in New Haven. I left the show profoundly moved, shaken. I had planned to have a late supper with friends, but I begged off and grabbed the first train back to New York. I wanted to be alone to savor that most exquisite thing, a great play truthfully and passionately acted. Later I looked at the printed version of the play, hoping to recapture something of what I had experienced that night in New Haven. To my amazed delight, it was all there on the page.

But how is this possible? The experience of a live play, as opposed to a play script, is so completely different. A performance is an event: it happens, unfolds in real time. The actors and the audience, live, together in a room or an arena, share a fiction they have agreed to believe is real. On the other hand, a piece of theater or a play written down is merely the transcript of an event. Stage directions *describe* action. Written dialogue *stands-in* for living voices. If a novel or short story is written to be read, a play is meant to be enacted. A good play-reader keeps this always in mind. It is the key to entering into the play. A scene or monologue on the page is only a beginning, the bare bones of a world, a map to somewhere else. It is the DNA of an eventual performance. But it is up to the reader to break the code and make the leap of imagination that brings the play to life.

On the page, a play is a puzzle to be cracked. With a novel, short story, or essay, you adopt the fixed point of view of the author. With a play, point of view comes unstuck. The reader plays all the parts, setting one voice off against another. The aim, and the fun, is in inhabiting another reality, and a good play, well read, is very much like a virtual reality. For me, no other reading experience is as engaging, as stimulating, as downright pleasurable as is piecing out a scene, monologue, or a song; placing it in the context of the setting or action suggested, and acting it out in my head.

Writings for the theater comprise a whole literature in themselves. And though no literature can claim to be older than comedy and drama, none relies more on the immediate and intimate, the truthful and the outrageous. After all, the point of theater is to have an effect on an audience. In his mid-teens, St. Augustine left his happy, stable, middle-class family and ran off to the Big City (in his case fourth-century Carthage), where, he says: "a cauldron of unholy lusts seethed and boiled within me." Stage plays particularly excited and disturbed him. However, he tells us, "if the play fails to touch the feelings of the audience, they go away disgusted, but if their feelings be touched, they sit it out raptly and shed tears of joy." All right, but how is this accomplished; this business of laughter and tears? What moves an audience? How do you hit the nerve? Twelve centuries later, Shakespeare suggests a pretty good answer when young Prince Hamlet remarks to the Players that "the purpose of playing" is to hold up a mirror, and show the "form and pressure" of the time. This is no vague ideal, but a statement of plain fact. We recognize ourselves in the conflicts and dilemmas on our stages. That is *why* we are moved. We sense our own time in the rhythms of the dialogue, the attitudes of the characters, and the action of a scene. Our plays are us.

This book is a sampling of some of the most remarkable voices of today's American theater. No anthology can hope to do more than scratch the surface of this vast, potent literature. But even a scratch exposes a rich vein of cultural and ethnic diversity, a mother lode of styles, structures, and forms of expression; satire, irony, farce, melodrama, realism, surrealism, magic-realism, to name just a few. My strategy has been to excerpt pieces of theater that can more or less stand on their own, and arrange them, matching and contrasting one with another. I have looked particularly for scripts that speak to the issues and interests of young adults. I take the view that coming of age means coming to realizations.

I hope this sampling will encourage the reader to search out the complete plays excerpted here, and go on to other works by these playwrights, and I hope she or he will be inspired to see some of these plays and to write plays of their own. If our theater is a reflection of us, of who we are—and it is—then the raw material for plays is all around us. Most of all, I hope the reader takes away an appreciation of the challenges, the fun, and the satisfaction in reading a play well.

Before each selection I have added information I believe the reader will find useful. (For biographical information about the playwrights see the notes that begin on page 163.) I've tried not to explain or to characterize the works I am introducing. That treat belongs to the reader.

# H<sub>I</sub>T-T<sub>H</sub>E-N<sup>E</sup>R<sub>V</sub>E

BY KATE ROTHSCHILD

**K**ate Rothschild makes a TV game show the subject of this sketch comedy. You might say that this is only fair. We have TV to thank for much of the recent increased interest in this very popular form of theater.

*Characters*

ELLIOT SIMPSON, the Host

LISA (16)

MELISSA (43), her mother

GERTRUDE (54)

SINDY (17), her daughter

*Lights up.*

*A typical game-show set with two podiums. The* HOST, ELLIOT SIMPSON, *sporting a loud jacket and a smarmy smile, addresses the audience.*

■　　■　　■

HOST: Hello out there and welcome to another fun-filled half-hour of "Hit-the-Nerve"—the game show where mothers and daughters compete to see who can provoke the quickest reaction. I'm Elliot Simpson, but you can think of me as your "emotional moderator." Now let's meet tonight's contestants. Hailing from Paramus, New Jersey, please welcome Lisa and her mother, Melissa.

(LISA, *age 16, and her mother,* MELISSA, *43, in identical lycra minidress ensembles, enter beaming.*)

HOST: Our returning five-time champions from Boston, Massachusetts . . . Gertrude and her daughter Sindy.

(GERTRUDE, *age 54, and her daughter* SINDY, *17, enter.* GERTRUDE *wears a prim skirt and sweater, while* SINDY*'s attire features ripped jeans and a tee shirt. They are bickering as they enter.*)

SINDY (*exasperated*): Mom, enough already.
GERTRUDE: Well, you almost gave me a heart attack. We could have been in an accident. (*To* HOST.) She's trying to kill me.
SINDY: I wasn't speeding!
HOST: Now, now, ladies. The game hasn't even started. No wonder you two are the champions.

(SINDY *assumes her natural scowl while a smiling* GERTRUDE *attempts, in vain, to brush her daughter's hair from her eyes. At the other podium,* LISA *and* MELISSA *are posing and primping, enjoying the spotlight.)*

HOST: OK, let's get right to the game. What are our categories tonight?

*(We hear an* ANNOUNCER*'s voice.)*

ANNOUNCER (*voice-over*): Elliot, our contentious categories tonight are . . .
"Appearance" . . .
"Listen to Your Mother" . . .
"Relationships" . . .
"Sex" . . .
and "When I Was Your Age" . . .

GERTRUDE (*shocked*): I am *not* discussing *sex* on national television!

SINDY: Mom, it's 1995. Lighten up.

GERTRUDE: In my day, we didn't even *talk* about it until we were married . . . you are still a virgin aren't you, Sindy?

SINDY (*mortified*): Mom!

HOST (*chuckling*): Gertrude, Sindy, now that's just shameless pandering to the judges. If you do it again there may be a penalty. OK ladies, you know how this works. You daughters pick a category, I give the mothers a topic and they go for the jugular. We'll start with our challengers. Lisa, pick a category.

LISA: "Appearance."

HOST: The topic is "clothes."

MELISSA: But I have no complaint with the way she looks.

LISA: That's because you dressed exactly like me.

MELISSA: It's not my fault I have the body of a sixteen-year-old.

LISA: Mother, you're forty-three.

MELISSA: Forty-two and a half. Anyway, we agreed that it would be cute to wear the same outfit.

LISA: Agreed? I never agreed to anything. It was *your* decision!

*(BUZZER sounds.)*

HOST: Well done, Melissa. Five points. Sindy?

SINDY: Uh . . . I'll take "Appearance" too.

GERTRUDE: Sindy, you sound so unsure of yourself. Be more assertive.

SINDY: I am assertive.

GERTRUDE: Then why are you slouching?

SINDY: I'm not slouching!

*(BUZZER sounds.)*

HOST: Whoa! Slow down there, ladies. I haven't given you a topic yet. The topic is "dressing appropriately."

GERTRUDE: "Dressing appropriately"? You mean like not wearing the Salvation Army fall collection on national television?

SINDY: What's wrong with the way I'm dressed?

GERTRUDE: It wouldn't have killed you to wear a skirt.

SINDY: I'm comfortable. I want to be judged by who I am.

GERTRUDE: A slob?

SINDY: I'll dress any way I want to. Stop trying to live my life for me!

(BUZZER *sounds.*)

HOST: Nicely done, ladies. We're finished with the first round so let's take a moment to meet our contestants. Lisa, Melissa, I hear that you two have shared some interesting mother-daughter experiences.

MELISSA: Yes Elliot, we have. Lisa and I posed for *Playboy* together.

HOST: Really?

MELISSA: They said we looked just like sisters.

LISA: Of course that was after she had the implants.

MELISSA: Lisa!

(BUZZER *sounds.*)

HOST: Hey, provoking a reaction from your mother . . . that's twenty-five bonus points, Lisa.

LISA: I wasn't trying.

(GERTRUDE *nudges* SINDY.)

GERTRUDE: See, she has the same problem you do. She just doesn't try.

SINDY: I *am* trying! You're never happy, are you?!!

(BUZZER *sounds.*)

HOST: Gertrude, I have to say. I've been doing this show for a long time but I've never seen anyone Hit-a-Nerve so quickly.

GERTRUDE: Thanks, Elliot. But I have to confess, Sindy's my third daughter. I have had a little practice.

HOST: And it shows.

MELISSA: Lisa's my only child. But she's really more like a pal. The truth is, we're only on the show to get more exposure for our dual modeling career.

GERTRUDE: What more do you have left to expose?

MELISSA (*to* GERTRUDE): Honey, if I was you, I'd keep it covered up too!

*(BELL rings.)*

HOST: Oh, Gertrude, I'm afraid that's a ten-point deduction. You just got a reaction from your challenger. It's your turn, Lisa.

LISA: How about "Relationships."

HOST: The topic is "boyfriends."

MELISSA: Hers or mine?

LISA: What's the difference?

MELISSA: And just what do you mean by that?

LISA: You stole Bobby from me.

MELISSA: The marriage never would have lasted.

LISA: You should know about marriages not lasting.

MELISSA: Why, you little bitch!

*(BUZZER sounds.)*

HOST: Oh boy, that was hitting hard, Lisa, but you've just scored another twenty reverse nerve-hitting bonus points. I'm beginning to wonder who's the mother and who's the daughter here.

LISA (*dripping with sarcasm*): Really?

MELISSA: And what's that supposed to mean?

LISA: You're not my sister and you're not my friend. You're my mother! (*Buries her head in her hands.*)

(BUZZER *sounds.*)

HOST: Five points. Good job, Melissa.

(MELISSA *puts her arms around* LISA.)

MELISSA: Honey, I never knew you felt this way. I . . . I guess you needed more guidance from me. Maybe I spent too much time trying to make you like me and not enough time trying to mold you into the perfect daughter.

LISA: A little nagging might have been nice.

MELISSA: I love you, Lisa.

LISA: I love you too, Mom. (*They hug.*)

(BELL *rings.*)

HOST: Uh-oh, a reconciliation. I'm afraid you two are disqualified.

MELISSA: What!?!

LISA: That's OK. Come on, I'll buy you a cheeseburger.

MELISSA: Now Lisa, you better stick with salad. You could afford to lose a few. (*Pats* LISA*'s stomach.*)

LISA (*indignant*): My weight is fine!

(BUZZER *sounds.*)

LISA: Thanks, Mom.

(MELISSA *and* LISA *exit arm in arm.*)

GERTRUDE: That's just so pathetic.

SINDY: At least Lisa's mother knows how to show affection.

GERTRUDE: What? You think I don't love you? Is that the problem?

SINDY: You don't respect me.

GERTRUDE: Of course I do.

SINDY (*touched*): Really?

HOST: Uh-oh. I think Sindy's about to forfeit the game.

GERTRUDE: Put a sock in it, Elliot.

HOST: Hey, I'm in charge here!

(BUZZER *sounds.*)

ANNOUNCER (*voice-over*): Congratulations, Mrs. Johnson. You got a reaction from the host.

SINDY: I'm so proud of you, Mom.

GERTRUDE: And I'm proud of you, dear. (*They hug.*)

(BELL *rings.*)

HOST: And our champions forfeit too. What a shame. Well, that's all for now. Good night and remember, it doesn't matter what you say, as long as you "Hit-the-Nerve!"

(*Lights out.*)

# "GIT ON BOARD"
## from *The Colored Museum*

BY GEORGE C. WOLFE

T*he Colored Museum* is a play of eleven "Exhibits." "Git on Board" begins the play. Here we have a dynamic mix of forms: part history, part satire, part disaster movie.

*Setting*

White walls and recessed lighting. A starkness befitting a museum where the myths and madness of black/Negro/colored Americans are stored.

Sound effects, music should be prerecorded, except for the drummer, who is live.

*Blackness. Cut by drums pounding. Then slides, rapidly flashing before us. Images we've all seen before, of African slaves being captured, loaded onto ships, tortured. The images flash, flash, flash. The drums crescendo. Blackout. And then lights reveal* MISS PAT, *frozen. She is black, pert, and cute. She has a flip to her hair and wears a hot pink miniskirt stewardess uniform.*

*She stands in front of a curtain which separates her from an offstage cockpit.*

*An electronic bell goes "ding" and* MISS PAT *comes to life, presenting herself in a friendly but rehearsed manner, smiling and speaking as she has done so many times before.*

■    ■    ■

MISS PAT: Welcome aboard Celebrity Slaveship, departing the Gold Coast and making short stops at Bahia, Port au Prince, and Havana, before our final destination of Savannah.

Hi. I'm Miss Pat and I'll be serving you here in Cabin A. We will be crossing the Atlantic at an altitude that's pretty high, so you must wear your shackles at all times. (*She removes a shackle from the overhead compartment and demonstrates.*)

To put on your shackle, take the right hand and close the metal ring around your left hand like so. Repeat the action using your left hand to secure the right. If you have any trouble bonding yourself, I'd be more than glad to assist.

Once we reach the desired altitude, the captain will turn off the Fasten Your Shackle sign . . . (*She efficiently points out the FASTEN YOUR SHACKLE signs on either side of her, which light up.*) . . . allowing you a chance to stretch and dance in the aisles a bit. But otherwise, shackles must be worn at all times.

(*The FASTEN YOUR SHACKLE signs go off.*)

MISS PAT: Also, we ask that you please refrain from call-and-response singing between cabins, as that sort of thing can lead to rebellion. And, of course, no drums are allowed on board. Can you repeat after me, "No drums." (*She gets the audience to repeat.*) With a little more enthusiasm, please. "No drums." (*After the audience repeats it.*) That was great!

Once we're airborne, I'll be by with magazines, and earphones can be purchased for the price of your firstborn male.

If there's anything I can do to make this middle passage more pleasant, press the little button overhead and I'll be with you faster than you can say, "Go down, Moses." (*She laughs at her "little joke."*) Thanks for flying Celebrity and here's hoping you have a pleasant takeoff.

(*The engines surge, the* FASTEN YOUR SHACKLE *signs go on, and over-articulate Muzak voices are heard singing as* MISS PAT *pulls down a bucket seat and "shackles-up" for takeoff.*)

VOICES:

> Get on board Celebrity slaveship
> Get on board Celebrity slaveship
> Get on board Celebrity slaveship
> There's room for many a more . . .

(*The engines reach an even, steady hum. Just as* MISS PAT *rises and replaces the shackles in the overhead compartment, the faint sound of African drumming is heard.*)

MISS PAT: Hi. Miss Pat again. I'm sorry to disturb you, but someone is playing drums. And what did we just say . . . "No drums." It must be someone in Coach. But we here in

Cabin A are not going to respond to those drums. As a matter of fact, we don't even hear them. Repeat after me. "I don't hear any drums." (*The audience repeats.*) And "I will not rebel."

*(The audience repeats. The drumming grows.)*

MISS PAT (*placating*): OK, now I realize some of us are a bit edgy after hearing about the tragedy on board *The Laughing Mary,* but let me assure you Celebrity has no intention of throwing you overboard and collecting the insurance. We value you!

*(She proceeds to single out individual passengers/audience members.)*

Why, the songs *you* are going to sing in the cotton fields, under the burning heat and stinging lash, will metamorphose and give birth to the likes of James Brown and the Fabulous Flames. And you, yes, *you,* are going to come up with some of the best dances. The best dances! The Watusi! The Funky Chicken! And just think of what *you* are going to mean to William Faulkner.

All right, so you're gonna have to suffer for a few hundred years, but from your pain will come a culture so complex. *And,* with this little item here ... (*She removes a basketball from the overhead compartment.*) ... you'll become millionaires!

*(There is a roar of thunder. The lights quiver and the FASTEN YOUR SHACKLE signs begin to flash.* MISS PAT *quickly replaces*

*the basketball in the overhead compartment and speaks very reassuringly.)*

MISS PAT: No, don't panic. We're just caught in a little thunderstorm. Now, the only way you're going to make it through is if you abandon your God and worship a new one. So, on the count of three, let's all sing. One, two, three . . .

Nobody knows de trouble I seen . . .

Oh, I forgot to mention, when singing, omit the *t-h* sound. "The" becomes "de." "They" becomes "dey." Got it? Good!

Nobody knows . . .

Nobody knows . . .

Oh, so you don't like that one? Well then let's try another—

Summer time and de livin' is easy . . .

Gershwin. He comes from another oppressed people so he understands.

Fish are jumpin' . . .

Come on.

And de cotton is high.

And de cotton is . . .

Sing, damnit!

*(Lights begin to flash, the engines surge, and there is wild drumming.* MISS PAT *sticks her head through the curtain and speaks with an offstage* CAPTAIN.*)*

MISS PAT: What?

VOICE OF CAPTAIN (*offstage*): Time warp!

MISS PAT: Time warp! (*She turns to the audience and puts on a pleasant face.*) The captain has assured me everything is fine. We're just caught in a little time warp. (*Trying to fight her growing hysteria.*) On your right you will see the American Revolution, which will give the U.S. of A. exclusive rights to your life. And on your left, the Civil War, which means you will vote Republican until FDR comes along. And now we're passing over the Great Depression, which means everybody gets to live the way you've been living. (*There is a blinding flash of light, and an explosion. She screams.*) Ahhhhhhhhh! That was World War I, which is not to be confused with World War II . . . (*There is a larger flash of light, and another explosion.*) . . . Ahhhhh! Which is not to be confused with the Korean War or the Vietnam War, all of which you will play a major role in.

Oh, look, now we're passing over the sixties. Martha and the Vandellas . . . *Julia* with Miss Diahann Carroll . . . Malcolm X . . . those five little girls in Alabama . . . Martin Luther King . . . Oh no! The Supremes broke up! (*The drumming intensifies.*) Stop playing those drums! Those drums will be confiscated once we reach Savannah. You can't change history! You can't turn back the clock! (*To the audience.*) Repeat after me, I don't hear any drums! I will not rebel! I will not rebel! I will not re—

(*The lights go out, she screams, and the sound of a plane landing and screeching to a halt is heard. After a beat, lights reveal a wasted, disheveled* MISS PAT, *but perky nonetheless.*)

MISS PAT: Hi. Miss Pat here. Things got a bit jumpy back there, but the captain has just informed me we have safely landed in Savannah. Please check the overhead before exiting, as any baggage you don't claim, we trash.

It's been fun, and we hope the next time you consider travel, it's with Celebrity.

*(Luggage begins to revolve onstage from offstage left, going past* MISS PAT *and revolving offstage right. Mixed in with the luggage are two male slaves and a woman slave, complete with luggage and ID tags around their necks.)*

MISS PAT (*with routine, rehearsed pleasantness*): Have a nice day. Bye-bye.

Button up that coat, it's kind of chilly.

Have a nice day. Bye-bye.

You take care now.

See you.

Have a nice day.

Have a nice day.

Have a nice day.

# "ARE YOU IN OR ARE YOU OUT?"

## from the musical revue *Paranoise*

MUSIC AND LYRICS BY SEAN HARTLEY

Early theater was narrative sung. The earliest actors chanted or sang their stories. When the subject was love, the hero would often have to answer a series of riddles or questions in order to win the hand of his beloved. If he answered incorrectly, all hope for love was lost, and plagues raged. In this heartbreaking, late twentieth century love song, the narrator must answer three questions. As in olden times, his answers will seal his fate.

*Setting*

Except for his accompanist, the singer is alone onstage

■  ■  ■

He said, "This is the deal, this is the way it's gotta be:
People must never know about you and me
We'll keep separate apartments, very discreet,
Whenever we meet on the street
I'll pretend you're just a friend"

Well, his mom was a Biddle
And his dad was the state attorney general
His aunt knew the queen and his brother was
    a Green Beret
I thought, "no wonder he's uptight,
But things will be all right in the end"

And his arms were strong and his teeth were white
And his hair was golden and his eyes were bright
And I'd never loved anyone who loved me too
So what was I to do?
He said, "Are you in or are you out?
Are you in or are you out?"
And there wasn't any doubt about it
I said, "In."

He said, "This is the deal,
This is the way it's gotta be:
You know that I've always wanted a family.
Well, I've finally found a woman who won't make any fuss,

She won't ask questions and she won't interfere with us.
We'll still see each other, just not as often as before.
Maybe we'll find we appreciate each other more.
At first it will seem strange,
But soon you'll see that nothing has to change."

And his arms were strong and his teeth were white
And his hair was golden and his eyes were bright
And he wanted me to tell him things would be okay
so what was I to say?
He said, "Are you in or are you out?
Are you in or are you out?"
And there wasn't any doubt about it
I said, "Out.

"Out with the lying and out with the games
Let's call things by their proper names
Out with pretending, get out of my life
Back in the closet, God pity your wife
Out with the hiding—must I go on?
Don't you get it?"
He said, "I got it."
And he was gone.

He said, "This is the deal, this is how life turned out to be:
I'm running out of hope on AZT.
Well, of course my wife divorced me, took the kids as well,
I see them once a month and the rest is hell.
I don't have much time left, maybe another year or two

and if you could stand it, I'd like to spend the time
  with you.
I know I made a mess of things, threw my life away,
I know that I should go but I want to stay."

And his teeth were yellow and his hair was gray
And he looked so weak I had to look away
And I knew he loved me, but I also knew
The pain he'd put me through
And he said, "Are you in or are you out?
Are you in or are you out?"
And I wanted to shout
"Get out!
Go away!"
But I said, "Stay."

# "HAIR ANONYMOUS GIRL LOOK IN THE MIRROR"
## from *Fires in the Mirror*

BY ANNA DEAVERE SMITH

**F**ires in the Mirror is a part of a series of performance pieces the playwright calls "On the Road: A Search for American Character." She creates these pieces "by interviewing people and later performing them, using their own words." Her goal she says "has been to find American character in the ways that people speak." Anna Deavere Smith shows how a single actor, by adopting the voices of different characters, can evoke an entire world by herself.

*Character* (appearing in this excerpt)

A teenaged black girl of Haitian descent

■  ■  ■

When I look in the mirror . . .
I don't know.
How did I find out I was Black . . .

*(Tongue sound.)*

When I grew up and I look in the mirror and saw I was
    Black.
When I look at my parents,
That's how I knew I was Black.
Look at my skin.
You Black?
Black is beautiful.
I don't know.
That's what I always say.
I think White is beautiful too.
But I think Black is beautiful too.
In my class nobody is White, everybody's Black,
and some of them is Hispanic.
In my class
you can't call any of them Puerto Ricans.
They despise Puerto Ricans, I don't know why.
They think that Puerto Ricans are stuck up and everything.
They say, Oh my Gosh my nail broke, look at that cute guy
    and everything.
But they act like that themselves.

They act just like White girls.
Black girls is not like that.
Please, you should be in my class.
Like they say that Puerto Ricans act like that
and they don't see that they act like that themselves.
Black girls, they do bite off the Spanish girls,
they bite off of your clothes.
You don't know what that means? biting off?
Like biting off somebody's clothes.
Like cop, following,
and last year they used to have a lot of girls like that.
They come to school with a style, right?
And if they see another girl with that style?
Oh my gosh look at her.
What she think she is,
she tryin' to bite off of me in some way
no don't be bitin' off of my sneakers
or like that.
Or doin' a hairstyle
I mean Black people are into hairstyles.
So they come to school, see somebody with a certain style,
they say uh-huh I'm gonna get me one just like that
    uh-huh,
that's the way Black people are
Yea-ah!
They don't like people doing that to them
and they do that to other people,
so the Black girls will follow the Spanish girls.
The Spanish girls don't bite off of us.
Some of the Black girls follow them.

But they don't mind
They don't care.
They follow each other.
Like there's three girls in my class,
they from the Dominican Republic.
They all stick together like glue.
They all three best friends.
They don't follow nobody,
like there's none of them lead or anything.
They don't hang around us either.
They're
by themselves.

# "Symphony of Rats"
## from *Unbalancing Acts*

BY RICHARD FOREMAN

**H**ere the playwright mixes the real and the surreal to create a world that is at once familiar and at the same time, very strange. The aim is to surprise, dislocate, unbalance the audience.

*Characters* (appearing in this excerpt)

VOICE, over loudspeaker

PRESIDENT

JEFF WEBSTER, presidential adviser

PEYTON, a mature lady

KATE VALK, a young woman

PRESIDENTIAL ASSISTANTS

*The play takes place in an area that is divided into two parts. One half seems to be a presidential sitting room, with a large fireplace and a felt-covered card table where presidential games are played. The mantel above the fireplace is wide enough for the actors to stand on, and a ladder leads up to it from the side. The other area is dominated by a presidential desk enclosed in a glass booth; a microphone sits on the desk, suggesting a secret broadcasting center. But the set is not realistic. Girders and other support systems dominate, plus there is much seemingly inappropriate decoration—gilded flowers festooned in corners, American flags, small paintings of flowers and telephones—as if it were a secret Pentagon operations center which had been decorated by an elderly, eccentric, and patriotic aunt of the President. Another noticeably bizarre element is the large, thick, brightly colored railings that subdivide the rooms. The walls are decorated with an assortment of wallpapers, with strange geometric objects painted over the wallpaper. This Pentagon control center has acquired distinct aspects of a child's playpen—which does not decrease its somberness and machinelike military qualities. The floor is painted in large geometric patterns. A presidential seal is visible on the floor, as well as on different sections of the wall. Many standing microphones are scattered about the set. More often than not, when the actors deliver their lines they speak into one of the microphones—all of which can be detached from their stands and may be carried about the stage. Usually, however, the actors do not detach the microphones, but come to the stands. These stands are unnaturally low, so that to speak into the microphone the actor is forced to bend his knees slightly and to angle his voice, as it were, into the mike.*

*JEFF, one of the presidential advisers, a tall man in a conservative business suit, is carefully laying out cards on the green felt tabletop as if he were going to read the cards to predict the future. He puffs on a pipe, contemplatively. KATE, a thin young woman in a floral print dress and a turban, enters and whispers to JEFF, then exits. The PRESIDENT slowly enters the room. Soft guitar music plays.*

■   ■   ■

VOICE (*from over a loudspeaker*): Ladies and gentlemen, the President of the United States.

*(The* PRESIDENT *glances at the audience, then comes to the table and sits at one side.* JEFF *sits at the other. The chairs are built to be as tall as barstools, but they lean forward slightly. The two men carefully adjust their pants, pulling their trousers up an inch to eliminate the stretching of fabric over the knees. Then they lift their feet slightly and the chairs tilt forward a bit more. At this time* PEYTON, *a mature lady in a black lace dress, smoking a cigar and wearing a cap with devil's horns, appears from nowhere and begins racing quickly around the room, making absolutely no noise, in a crouched position like a devilish Groucho Marx. She is outside the two men's line of vision. They do not turn their heads as the* PRESIDENT *frowns slightly and speaks very quietly to* JEFF.*)*

PRESIDENT: Do you hear something?
JEFF (*He speaks with an accent throughout the play.*): No.
PRESIDENT: Funny.

*(The* PRESIDENT *rises and begins to slowly look about the room. He doesn't see* PEYTON *even though she now crosses directly in front of him. The* PRESIDENT *goes slowly to a microphone center stage.* PEYTON *has arrived behind a wooden pillar. She leans out provocatively, puffing on her cigar.)*

PEYTON: Hey—wanna go someplace special?

*(She runs off, leaving the* PRESIDENT *alone at the mike. He thinks for a while, then begins to speak into the microphone as if talking to himself, though he is addressing the audience.)*

PRESIDENT: What's out there in space? (*Pause.*) Jesus, you've been there. What's out there? Silence. Vast silence? (*Pause.*) There are . . . complex webs of radiations all through space, aren't there? Yes? (*Pause.*) Isn't that silence a kind of noise? Not for the human ear perhaps. (*Pause.*) I guess I'm projecting my own thoughts. True, I haven't been there.

JEFF (*bending into a mike at his table*): True.

PRESIDENT (*pause*): So you say . . . vast silence.

JEFF: Yes.

PRESIDENT (*pause*): Vast silence.

JEFF: Yes.

PRESIDENT: Anything else? (*Pause.*) No. That should be enough for me. You're trying to make a point.

JEFF: No. (*Pause.*) I've made my point, Mr. President.

PRESIDENT (*pause*): Am I now in outer space? Why of course I am. I'm on Earth, but that's still . . . space.

*(Pause. As he thinks this over,* PEYTON—*now without her devil's cap or cigar—reemerges as a sedate presidential adviser. Without the* PRESIDENT *noticing her, she and* JEFF *whisper behind his back.)*

Ladies and gentlemen, Earth . . . exists in outer space, doesn't it? Yes. So I'm in outer space. (*Pause.*) I don't have to get in a rocket ship to be in outer space. No. I'm in outer space now. (*Pause.*) What am I aware of? Vast silence?

JEFF: Is that what you're aware of, Mr. President?

PRESIDENT (*pause*): I don't know.

(PEYTON *comes forward, smiling faintly, and gives a golf club to the* PRESIDENT *as several presidential assistants enter with clubs of their own. The assistants line up in the rear to practice their swings. The* PRESIDENT *takes his club, crosses to the glass booth, climbs on the presidential broadcast desk, and inside the glass booth tries to swing, banging into the sides of the booth and generally becoming tangled and disheveled.*)

PEYTON: Got a problem with your swing, Mr. President?

PRESIDENT: It don't mean a thing.

JEFF (*sucking calmly at his pipe*): Ah. A problem with a swing don't mean a thing. Not a thing. It don't mean a thing.

PEYTON: A problem with a swing is a big thing. (*She sings, very softly, addressing the audience.*)

'Cause it don't mean a thing

If it ain't got that swing.

(*Explains to the audience.*) Ladies and gentlemen. He in the emotional foreground got a problem with his swing. It's a big thing. A real big thing. All the others, they do okay. No problems, no beefs. A swing about which to sing.

PRESIDENT (*climbing down from the booth*): Golf my ass.

JEFF: It isn't the game of golf, Mr. President. It's a bigger game. The swing is the thing. But it isn't a game of golf, Mr. President. Not at all.

*(The* PRESIDENT *is now at the rear with the other golfers. As he addresses his imaginary ball, a golf pro uses a little stick to try and prod him into better form.)*

JEFF *(downstage, barking out commands)*: Pull back here, Mr. President. Out here. Twist more here.

PRESIDENT *(irritated, pulling away from the pro)*: Look—

JEFF: Look my ass, Mr. President. *(He makes a slightly obscene gesture using his fist.)*

PRESIDENT: Ah, it's a wise man making a mental muscle.

JEFF: Are you into golf, Mr. President, or are you into a very significant hallucination?

PRESIDENT: I don't know what I'm into. *(He's bent over, leaning against a post.)*

PEYTON: *(Standing behind the* PRESIDENT, *she somehow produces a golf ball from between his legs.)* Hit the ball OUT OF the hole, Mr. President.

PRESIDENT: That's ass-backwards.

JEFF: Why not do the impossible, Mr. President?

PEYTON: Hey, wanna go someplace special?

JEFF and PEYTON *(singing softly)*:

> It don't mean a thing
> if it ain't got that swing
> doo wop doo wop
> bop bop bop.

PRESIDENT: *(He's crossed to the booth and sits at his desk, addressing the nation over the radio.)* You'll find this hard to believe. I've gotten messages from outer space. In my official capacity, these messages have come through to me. They reveal to me that the end of our world approaches. But I'm afraid to reveal this information . . . to my contemporaries. I feel I can't reveal it openly. It's a question of the mental well-being of millions of weak, fallible people for whom I feel responsible. But it's eating me up inside, knowing this, not being able to reveal this.

PEYTON: Perhaps what's required of you is a certain kind of spiritual effort, Mr. President.

PRESIDENT: Spiritual effort . . . ? I don't know specifically what you mean.

*(He leaves his booth to rejoin them, accidentally running into a pillar and getting a good knock on the head.)*

PEYTON *(paying no attention to the* PRESIDENT*'s collision)*: Unconsciously you know. Why fight it, Mr. President?

PRESIDENT *(holding his head)*: Listen, this is eating me up inside. How can I pretend to myself it hasn't really happened?

PEYTON: Ah, that means you imagined it, and it happened.

PRESIDENT: I'm taking a vacation.

PEYTON: Beginning now?

PRESIDENT *(moves to a mike)*: I have the option whenever I want the option. Here I go.

*(*KATE *reenters and all line up behind the mikes to do a kind of recitation as the music, which until now has been repeated phrases of a romantic violin, becomes a lively piano bounce.)*

PEYTON: Mr. President! If you go out the front—

*(She breaks off, in the hopes that the* PRESIDENT *can complete her phrase, but all he seems able to do is stutter "Do-o-o—.")*

KATE and JEFF: Door!

PEYTON: I'll surprise you with a big hello, hello
And you'll think I'm shouting from the upstairs window,
But really
It'll be in your OWN head.

PRESIDENT (*interjecting*): Did I leave the room?

PEYTON: If you sit in the invisible easy chair
I'll make REAL cookies and milk
So intense
Your head'll spin.

PRESIDENT: Did I lose my watch?

PEYTON: If you turn out all the lights,
I'll scream fire
And you'll suddenly be able
To see in the dark.

PRESIDENT (*taking out his wallet, perplexed*): Whose money is this?

PEYTON: If you open a drawer . . .

PRESIDENT: Did you say door?

PEYTON: Drawer.

PRESIDENT: Did I open a drawer?

PEYTON: Did you say DOOR?

PRESIDENT: Drawer.

PEYTON: DOOR?

*(The recitation breaks down.* KATE *approaches the* PRESIDENT *and grabs his hand, which he repeatedly pulls away.)*

PRESIDENT: No. Once upon a man. A time. Once upon a time, a man. He held out his hand to receive a gift. It was slapped into his hand. It was something to eat. (KATE *bites his hand and the* PRESIDENT *screams in pain.)* It hurt. It hurt. It hurt. (KATE *holds up a small card with a picture of a tiger painted on it.)* My mental Polaroid is broken. I snap a picture, but nothing happens.

KATE (*smiling softly, strangely*): Where do I come from, Mr. President?

PRESIDENT: Another planet? Why did I say that?

PEYTON: Guess why.

KATE: (*She carries a tray loaded with fruits and vegetables which she holds out toward the* PRESIDENT. *Very romantic violin music rises.)* There is no food, Mr. President. This food is artificially created.

PRESIDENT: But you've just shown me a tray of—

KATE: This planet has, through the lack of foresight and self-ishness of its inhabitants, exhausted its natural resources, its ability to bear fruit and feed the population of humans and animals. So this food you see has been artificially cre-ated. (*The* PRESIDENT *takes an apple and eats a bite, thoughtfully, as in the rear a magic cabinet rolls onstage. He suddenly reacts as if the apple tasted terrible.)* I will tell you how food is created.

PRESIDENT: But that's self-evident. It has nothing to do with my problems at the moment.

KATE: Only . . . women are able to create this food. Placing themselves in certain, specially designed containers.

(PEYTON *is seen inside the cabinet, holding out her arms to invite the whole world. The cabinet revolves, opening and closing its doors, as* KATE *circles it once then returns to speak to the* PRESIDENT.)

PRESIDENT (*as the cabinet revolves*): This is . . . very interesting.

KATE: They are able to project thought-beams to a radio absorption center in space.

PRESIDENT: In space. You mean it's possible?

KATE: Only women are able to do this. It is difficult for them to explain what they are doing. But this is the way food is created.

PRESIDENT: In the earth, the soil?

KATE: It grows in the earth, as before. Of course. But it is now understood as an artificial, willed process which depends upon the concentration of mind energy of millions of women all over the globe, in unison.

PRESIDENT: But how?

KATE: They project certain rays from within these resonating chambers . . .

PRESIDENT (*pointing to the cabinet*): Those?

KATE: . . . fructifying the earth through the multiple exchange of high-energy brain waves.

PRESIDENT: This is . . . highly interesting.

PEYTON (*speaking into a microphone from inside the cabinet*): The method itself was discovered in simultaneous moments of mystical revelation occurring simultaneously to twenty-five women of different nationalities and ages, throughout the globe, years ago during the depth of the world food supply exhaustion and resulting famine. Remember?

PRESIDENT: Well, uh . . . yes, I . . .

PEYTON: All historically recorded but now, alas, a legend rather than reality.

PRESIDENT: It's true, we have plenty to eat, seemingly.

KATE (*in a trance*): And women, thousands upon thousands all across the planet, do this thing. They make the earth fruitful, even though the exact mechanism of this thing is not known. It is done through faith, love . . . and the imagination!

*(Mystical music rises.)*

PRESIDENT: The imagination, you say.

KATE: Yes, Mr. President.

PRESIDENT: I regret to say that's a realm into which the deeper I delve, the more problematic . . .

KATE: Really?

PRESIDENT: Yes, really.

KATE: You could be hiding from something, Mr. President.

# from GREATER TUNA

## BY JASTON WILLIAMS, JOE SEARS, AND ED HOWARD

**W**hen we uncover the weirdness in the lives of our small towns, we discover their humor. It seems the harder we laugh the greater is our affection for them. This is an idea American theater has taken from the popular radio comedies of the 1930s and '40s.

In the original production of *Greater Tuna*, all the denizens of Tuna, Texas, were played by two actors.

*Characters* (appearing in this excerpt)

BERTHA BUMILLER

JODY BUMILLER

STANLEY BUMILLER

CHARLENE BUMILLER

CHAD HARTFORD

■   ■   ■

BERTHA (*offstage*): Charlene! Stanley! Don't make me call you
   again. (BERTHA *enters and turns off radio.*) Jody, honey. Get in
   here and finish your breakfast. (JODY *enters.*) Jody, honey,
   you want some more oatmeal?

JODY: No, Mama.

BERTHA: How 'bout some of these biscuits and gravy, honey;
   you hardly even touched 'em.

JODY: I already had some, Mama.

BERTHA: Well, baby, I could fry you some more bacon.

JODY: Mama, I don't want nothin'.

BERTHA: Is there something wrong with them hash browns?

JODY: No, Mama.

BERTHA: Well, have some more—Jody, what's that out there on
   the back porch? Oh, no! No, Jody, you didn't. Uh-uh! I will
   not have another puppy!

JODY: Mama, it followed me home.

BERTHA: From where?

JODY: From Petey Fisk's.

BERTHA: That Petey Fisk has given you another dog. He saves
   the dogs of the world and sends them home for me to
   feed. Well, you can't have another dog. Eight dogs is too
   many. You cannot have another dog, Little Jody.

JODY: I'll take care of it, Mama.

BERTHA: Honey, it's not a matter of takin' care of it. It's not normal. It's not normal for you to have eight to ten dogs fol-
   lowin' you all the time, and don't let that dog in the house.
   That reporter from Houston will be here any minute. (JODY

*exits and changes to* STANLEY.) I said, don't let that . . . now isn't that the cutest little thing . . . Awwoohhh, get down. Quit. Stop it . . . He's done it to me again. He has done it to me again. Come on, you. Yes, you . . . Come on and get out there with the rest of 'em. I gotta set for an interview. (*To the other dogs.*) Get away from that door! All of you! Get back! (*She lets the dog out.*) Now come on, you. You sweet thing. Now y'all let her alone. Bless her heart, isn't she cute? . . . I could kill that Goddamned Petey Fisk! (STANLEY *enters.*) Stanley, honey, you want some oatmeal?

STANLEY: Un-uh.

BERTHA: Well, honey, how 'bout some of those biscuits?

STANLEY: Un-uhhhh.

BERTHA: Will you try some hash browns?

STANLEY: Oh, Mama, get off—I'll get some M&M's on the way to trade school.

BERTHA: Stanley, man cannot live by M&M's alone.

STANLEY: Oh, Mama, get off!

BERTHA: And don't you lie to me about trade school. Vera Carp said you spent half the morning yesterday sitting in your car out in front of the grocery store.

STANLEY: Well, Vera Carp can kiss my rusty butt.

BERTHA: Stanley, don't you start.

STANLEY: Mama, I'd be just fine if Charlene would stop it.

BERTHA: I wish to God that you and your sister would stop that fighting!

STANLEY: Yeah . . . I heard her up there groanin'.

BERTHA: Stanley, she'll hear you.

STANLEY: Locks the door, turns on the water, starts groanin'.

BERTHA: Stanley!

STANLEY: Every time the groanin' starts, I know she's tryin' to squeeze into another pair of my blue jeans.

BERTHA: Now Stanley, you may be big yourself someday.

STANLEY: If I am—shoot me.

BERTHA: Stanley!

STANLEY: Mama, she ripped out three pair of Wranglers in the last month.

BERTHA: Charlene! Charlene, I know you can hear me. Get out of Stanley's jeans now!

STANLEY: Yeah, her hips are so big she has to lay down on the bed and groan into them.

BERTHA: Stanley, will you stop it! Now we're gonna find her a good diet.

STANLEY: You better find her a good surgeon.

BERTHA: Stanley! Get out of here before you drive me to a rubber room at Big Springs! Charlene! Charlene! You get out of Stanley's jeans. You know you're too big to fit in 'em. It just breaks my heart to hurt that baby's feelings.

STANLEY (*as he exits*): Yeah . . . I shoulda known you'd take her side. (STANLEY *changes to* CHARLENE.)

BERTHA: Stanley, don't let those dogs in the house! Get out of here!! . . . Thunder, get off that chair; you know better. You better get out that door. Look at this mess, and I just cleaned this house. Oh, my God, Bingo, what is that? Oh, no! Get out of here! Now wait. Come back here and take that with you! Go on, get out! You dogs are gonna be the death of me . . . Charlene! Charlene, honey, will you hurry up! I know you're working on your poem for the radio show, but sweetheart, your breakfast is getting cold.

CHARLENE (*offstage*): Mama! Come up here and get this dog out of my room!

BERTHA: Which one?

CHARLENE (*offstage*): Woffie.

BERTHA: Woffie, come down here. Get on down here. (*Whistles.*) Come on, Woffie . . . Now listen you—I told you about comin' through that door . . . the next time, I said the next time you come in this house, I know a German Shepherd that's gonna be lookin' for a new home. (*Points to another dog.*) And you're next! (CHARLENE *enters.*) Charlene, honey, you want some oatmeal?

CHARLENE: No.

BERTHA: Well, how 'bout some biscuits?

CHARLENE: Un-uh.

BERTHA: Will you try some hash browns?

CHARLENE: No, thank you.

BERTHA: Well, here honey, at least have a cup of coffee. (CHARLENE *repeatedly scoops sugar into her cup, making sound effects.*) Charlene. Charlene, honey, now stop! Remember that agreement we made that we were gonna use Sweet and Slender in our coffee?

CHARLENE: I used Sweet and Slender when I still had something to live for, Mother.

BERTHA: Oh, honey, what's wrong?

CHARLENE: Nothin'!

BERTHA: Why are you mad?

CHARLENE: I'm not!

BERTHA: Charlene, snap! Now honey, everybody can't be cheerleader.

CHARLENE: Oh, Mother . . .

BERTHA: Well, honey, there are other things to live for.

CHARLENE: Name one.

BERTHA: Well, I can't think of any right now, but when I do I'll write 'em down and give 'em to you.

CHARLENE: I'll tell you one thing. If that vicious little Connie Carp calls me "two-bits" one more time, she better send out for bandages.

BERTHA: She's just like her mother. You kill her with kindness.

CHARLENE: I'll kill her with somethin'!

BERTHA: You do unto others . . .

CHARLENE (*as she exits*): Uh-huh! (CHARLENE *changes to* CHAD.)

BERTHA: And don't let those damn dogs in the house! Get out of here! I wish you would get on that table! Please get on that table! Trixie, Trixie, Dolly, now come on honey, get out. You girls know better. Woffie! You come through that door one more time and you'll need drugs to kill the pain! Now I have had it! (*We hear* CHAD HARTFORD *offstage, ringing a* DOORBELL.) Oh, it's that reporter. Comin'! (*She checks her appearance.* RINNNNNGGG!) I said I was comin'! (RINNNNNGGGGGG!) Well, you'll just have to hold onto your horses! I said I was comin'! (RINNNGGG. RINNNGGGG. RINNNGGGG. CHAD *enters.*) Yes?

CHAD: Mrs. Bumiller?

BERTHA: Yes.

CHAD: My name is Chad Hartford.

BERTHA: Oh, come in, Mr. Hartford. Could I get you somethin' to drink? A cup of coffee?

CHAD: I don't care for anything to drink. I'm in a bit of a hurry. Could we get right to the interview?

BERTHA: Well, certainly.

CHAD: Now, you are chairing the Censorship of the Text Books Committee, am I correct?

BERTHA: Oh, no no no no. That's the Reverend Spikes who heads that committee . . . although I am a member. We're gonna have a meetin' this afternoon by the way. But please, don't come. The Reverend Spikes, he just hates the press. I think it's because of all those old folks' homes he owns, and all them terrible things they said about him in the newspapers. Well, I better shut up. Anyway, I head the subcommittee that wants to snatch the books off the shelves of the local high school library. Some of those books are absolutely disgusting. Our children have no business reading them, and somebody has got to protect the minds of the children.

CHAD: Before we get to the books, Mrs. Bumiller, could you tell me what in your background do you feel qualifies you to censor library books?

BERTHA: Well, I can briefly list my activities, if you like.

CHAD: Please.

BERTHA: Well, I'm currently president of the Ladies for a Better Tuna. I am den mother for Den 225. I'm the only high-C soprano in the First Baptist Choir. And I'm currently recorder of the Javalina Club; that's a women's auxiliary of the Wild Hogs. It's kind of a break-off of the Lions Club. We just thought the Lions were too liberal. I'm the former head of the local B.B.B., that's the Better Baptist Bureau. And I'm a member of our shut-in visiting squad, the Tuna Helpers. And I'm currently president and cofounder of Citizens for Fewer Blacks in Literature.

CHAD: Thank you, Mrs. Bumiller. I think I get the idea.

BERTHA: Well, all right.

CHAD: Now, exactly what are the books that you think should be removed from the shelves?

BERTHA: Well, now there's four of 'em that we're gonna try and have removed nationwide. And then we're gonna go from there.

CHAD: What are the four books, Mrs. Bumiller?

BERTHA: *Roots.* Now, we don't deny that *Roots* has been a very popular TV series, but we feel it only shows one side of the slavery issue.

CHAD: Go on . . .

BERTHA: *Bury My Heart at Wounded Knee.* Well, it's the most disgusting title to begin with; it just makes me want to erp. It villifies a great American, General Custer. And it encourages the reader to believe that the United States Government can't be trusted in makin' any treaties.

CHAD: What's next?

BERTHA: *Huckleberry Finn,* by Mark Twain.

CHAD: Did he write that?

BERTHA: Uh-huh. Now, that book shows a preteenage boy avoidin' his chores, runnin' away from home, cohortin' with a Negro convict, and puttin' on women's clothes.

CHAD: Go on . . .

BERTHA: *Romeo and Juliet.*

CHAD: What, pray tell, is wrong with *Romeo and Juliet?*

BERTHA: It just shows sex among teenagers, that's all. And we're not for that, and we're certainly not going to encourage it. Besides, it shows a rampant disrespect for parental authority.

CHAD: You are aware that William Shakespeare wrote that play?

BERTHA: Oh, yes we are. And we're lookin' into the rest of his stuff, too. He wrote *Barefoot in the Park,* didn't he?

CHAD (*pause*): Mrs. Bumiller, quite often these days, people claim to talk to God. Do you talk to God?

BERTHA: Well, I pray.

CHAD: I didn't ask you that, Mrs. Bumiller. I asked if you talk to God directly?

BERTHA: Well, no, I don't. But he leaves little messages for me . . . with the Reverend Spikes. And secondhand messages from the Lord is good enough for me.

CHAD: Thank you, Mrs. Bumiller. I think we got one hell of a story here.

BERTHA: Don't you rush off. I've got other interesting things to tell you about Tuna.

CHAD: Well, I'm sure it just boggles the mind, Mrs. Bumiller, but I really must run.

BERTHA: Now, wait a minute. What was the name of your magazine?

CHAD: *Intellect.*

BERTHA: I don't believe we have that here in Tuna.

CHAD: I'll see that you get a copy. Good-bye, Mrs. Bumiller. (CHAD *exits and changes to* PETEY.*)

BERTHA: Well, bye. Well, I think reporters just ask the silliest questions. Well, I guess I'm lucky he didn't ask more than he did. Thank God he didn't ask me about my family. Poor Charlene. That girl, she's just going crazy over not getting

* Petey is a later character in the play.

cheerleader. I said, "Charlene, honey, settle down, it'll be fine. You'll get cheerleader next year." And she looks at me with tears streaming down her cheeks and says, "Mama, I'm a senior." I don't know how to tell my only daughter she's never gonna be a cheerleader. I just don't know how to do it. Oooohhh, and Stanley. I swear I don't know what I'm gonna do with that boy, datin' that Mexican girl. He never has been right. Oh, but Jody's going to be OK, except that he's got eight to ten dogs following him all the time, but he'll grow out of that. I know he will. I hope. (BERTHA *takes out knife and begins to prepare vegetables.*) At least I didn't have to lie about Hank. I swear, I've cooked and cleaned for that sorry son of a bitch . . . for twenty-seven years, and he won't even take me to the drive-in movies. Of course, I pretend not to notice as we go to church on Sunday morning, after Saturday night. After I've smelled the perfume and seen the lipstick smears. I swear, sometimes I just wish that man would have a stroke! I swear I do! . . . I don't mean that . . . God, forgive me. I don't mean that. I am so glad that reporter didn't ask.

# from FOB (Prologue)

BY DAVID HENRY HWANG

This award-winning, groundbreaking work of Asian-American theater examines the stresses and tensions within one culture rather than between groups or ethnicities.

*Character*

DALE, an American of Chinese descent, second generation, in his early twenties

*Time*
1978

*Setting*
The back room of a small Chinese restaurant in Torrance, California

*Lights up on a blackboard. Enter* DALE *dressed preppie. The blackboard is the type that can flip around so both sides can be used. He lectures like a university professor, using the board to illustrate his points.*

■ ■ ■

DALE: F-O-B. Fresh Off the Boat. FOB. What words can you think of that characterize the FOB? Clumsy, ugly, greasy FOB. Loud, stupid, four-eyed FOB. Big feet. Horny. Like Lenny in *Of Mice and Men*. Very good. A literary reference. High-water pants. Floods, to be exact. Someone you wouldn't want your sister to marry. If you are a sister, someone you wouldn't want to marry. That assumes we're talking about boy FOBs, of course. But girl FOBs aren't really as . . . FOBish. Boy FOBs are the worst, the . . . pits. They are the sworn enemies of all ABC—oh, that's "American Born Chinese"—of all ABC girls. Before an ABC girl will be seen on Friday night with a boy FOB in Westwood, she would rather burn off her face. (*He flips around the board. On the other side is written: "1. Where to find FOBs. 2. How to spot a FOB."*) FOBs can be found in great numbers almost anyplace you happen to be, but there are some locations where they cluster in particularly large swarms. Community colleges, Chinese-club discos, Asian sororities, Asian fraternities, Oriental churches, shopping malls, and, of course, Bee Gee concerts. How can you spot a FOB? Look out! If you can't answer that, you might be one. (*He flips back the board, reviews.*) F-O-B. Fresh Off the Boat. FOB. Clumsy, ugly, greasy FOB. Loud, stupid, four-eyed FOB. Big feet. Horny. Like Lenny in *Of Mice and Men*. Floods. Like Lenny in *Of Mice and Men*. F-O-B. Fresh Off the Boat. FOB. (*Lights fade to black. We hear American pop music, preferably in the funk—R&B—disco area.*)

# "EQUITY"
## from *Reachin'*

BY CYNTHIA L. COOPER

**B**y isolating or caricaturing events in our daily lives, theater helps us see the games we play, and how we often manipulate others. No environment provides more material for this kind of theater than high school.

*Characters*

ROB, male

NIKKI, female

JEANNIE, female

*Reachin'* is a play of several interconnected skits. The play can be performed by a minimum of three actors—two women and one man. The actors do not necessarily perform the same character from sketch to sketch, and in some sketches may play more than one character.

ROB—*in sunglasses—leans as if standing against a locker. He watches people go by.*

■ ■ ■

ROB: Buzz—that's my teacher, Mr. Buzinsky, we call him Buzz—Buzz says to me this morning that there aren't enough en-roll-EEs in the construction class. He says Fuzz—that's the principal, Mr. Fuzio—says the class has to be canceled.

(ROB *rips off his sunglasses, and lurches up, reenacting his discussion with* BUZZ.)

"What do you mean, man! This is the best, the only, the main 'be there' class in the whole joint. This is why I'm in school, man! Has Fuzz lost his neurons or what is it, man?" (*Relaxing, gesticulating.*) Well, Buzz just looked at me and said he was sorry, he'd tried everything he could think of. He even sent some flyers around and went and talked to a bunch of scuzz—those are ninth graders, scuzz, we call 'em—and he couldn't get hardly any guys to sign up. (*Animated.*) So I said: "Guys? . . . Hold on there a minute, man . . . you're giving me an I-DE-a. The problem with you and Fuzz, Buzz, is you are out of what it is. You just leave it to Cuzz"—that's me, Cuzz,—'cuz . . . well, 'cuz I'm a thinking man.

(ROB *relaxes. He puts the sunglasses on, leans against the locker again.* NIKKI *walks by.*)

NIKKI (*somewhat flirtatiously*): Hi, Cuzz.

ROB: There you are, my fav. I've been looking all over the joint for you.

NIKKI: Looks to me like you've been standing right there most of the morning.

ROB: Well, I have been pondering somethin' 'cuz . . . well, just 'cuz. And I have formulated a question you may be able to help me with, Nikki.

NIKKI: Sure.

ROB: Well, I have one problem. I am in this supercharged class taught by Buzz . . .

NIKKI: Construction?

ROB: The very same. And . . . This class is overloaded with guys . . . turning guys away. But I finally said to Buzz, and Buzz said to Fuzz, I said, "Buzz, I'm lonely in this here class, 'cuz there is not a single female presence. As an adolescent, I cannot be de-PRIVED in this way of a female presence."

NIKKI: That's one of those vo-ed things, isn't it?

ROB: The same. But somethin' special. That's why I'm in it. And Buzz says to me, he says, "Cuzz, I'm sorry, we can't allow girls in this class . . . there's too much dangerous equipment and all. When you're constructing an entire house from ground up—foundation to roof—you can't have any girls around."

NIKKI: Are you kidding? Did he say that to you? I'm reporting this to Fuzz. "Dangerous equipment." That's outrageous, Cuzz.

ROB: Keep listening. So, I said, "Buzz, girls can learn how to use equipment. That's not too cool, man." So Buzz agrees with me, but he says, "Construction takes stamina. Girls don't have that."

NIKKI: I don't be-LIEVE this! This is totally incredible.

ROB: Don't I know it? I said, "Buzz, you're out of touch, man 'cuz I know a whole lot of the feminine persuasion that could do a whole lot better than some of the scuzz you let in this class." And I said, "Why shouldn't a girl get training for a job that'll earn top dollar . . . like a guy? What do you think, Buzz, that girls don't want a nice car and to be looking good? What do you think, Buzz—that a girl's gonna just cut outta high school and go have babies? That's history, man."

NIKKI: Yeah! I ought to go find him and tell him a thing or two myself.

ROB: There's more. I said, "It's people like you, Buzz, that hold back all the women . . . and when you hold back women you hold back all of us. A woman's got to be independent, too; can't be relying on someone else who might keel over some morning before the Wheaties are served. What do you think, man, that girls are always going to be happy earning sixty percent of what guys do? That girls are always going to be happy working in some pink-collar ghetto, being low person on the office directory, having to be twice as good to get half as far?"

NIKKI: You really told him, Cuzz . . . man, that's great! Why'd you do all that?

ROB: 'Cuz.

NIKKI: So he backed down, huh?

ROB: Naw. He told me it didn't matter what I said, the girls in our school didn't have the guts to sign up for construction, and I just better get used to it being all guys. So drop it, Cuzz, he said.

NIKKI: He doesn't think any girls in this school are tough enough to sign up?

ROB: I am giving to you what's inside quotation marks. That's what I was hoping to ask you, Nikki. What else can I say to Buzz?

NIKKI: You don't have to say another word, Cuzz.

ROB: I don't think I'm following.

NIKKI: I'll show him who isn't tough enough! If I can stand on my feet ten hours at a shot at the restaurant for minimum wage, I think I'm plenty tough enough to pound a few nails into a few boards for a lot more bucks.

ROB: Well, I wasn't going to say, but I thought you could handle it . . .

NIKKI: Darn right, I can. I'm going over to Mr. Buzinsky's room right now, and I'm telling him I'm signing up for construction whether he likes it or not. Let him put that bit in his drill for a while.

ROB: Yeah . . . well, if you think you're up to it . . .

NIKKI: Cuzz—don't worry about this. I know how to handle his type. Thanks for telling me, okay?

ROB: Yeah, sure, got it.

(NIKKI *exits.* ROB *jumps in a little "yahoo," and then leans back against the locker, sunglasses on.*)

JEANNIE (*flirtatiously*): Hi, Cuzz.

ROB: Hey, there you are. I've been looking all over the joint for you.

JEANNIE: Oh yeah? What'd ya want?

ROB: Well, you know Mr. Buzinsky . . . teaches construction?

JEANNIE: Yeah.

ROB: Well, I just had this outrageous encounter with him. See, what happened is I told him I needed a little feminine diver-SITY . . .

(ROB *puts his arm around* JEANNIE *and they exit, as* ROB*'s voice fades, and we hear* JEANNIE *saying "No!" "I don't believe it . . ." etc.*)

# "WORDS, WORDS, WORDS"

## from *All in the Timing*

> **D**avid Ives is famous for his wordplay. Just as in rap, where words set to rhythms give us a look at new uses of language, here the playwright gleefully examines the old saw that three monkeys, typing into infinity, will eventually produce *Hamlet*.

*Characters*

MILTON, a boy monkey

SWIFT, a boy monkey

KAFKA, a girl monkey

> *Lights come up on three monkeys pecking away at three type-writers. Behind them, a tire-swing is hanging. The monkeys are named* MILTON, SWIFT *and* KAFKA. KAFKA *is a girl monkey.*
>
> *They shouldn't be in monkey suits, by the way. Instead, they wear the sort of little-kid clothes that chimps wear in circuses: white shirts and bow ties for the boys, a flouncy little dress for* KAFKA.

*They type for a few moments, each at his own speed. Then* MILTON *runs excitedly around the floor on his knuckles, swings onto the tire-swing, leaps back onto his stool, and goes on typing.* KAFKA *eats a banana thoughtfully.* SWIFT *pounds his chest and shows his teeth, then goes back to typing.*

SWIFT: I don't know. I just don't know . . .

KAFKA: Quiet, please. I'm trying to concentrate here. (*She types a moment with her toes.*)

MILTON: Okay, so what've you got?

SWIFT: Me?

MILTON: Yeah, have you hit anything? Let's hear it.

SWIFT (*reads what he's typed*): "Ping-drobba fft fft fft inglewarp carcinoma." That's as far as I got.

KAFKA: I like the "fft fft fft."

MILTON: Yeah. Kind of onomatopoeic.

SWIFT: I don't know. Feels to me like it needs some punching up.

MILTON: You can always throw in a few jokes later on. You gotta get the through line first.

SWIFT: But do you think it's *Hamlet?*

MILTON: Don't ask me. I'm just a chimp.

KAFKA: They could've given us a clue or something.

SWIFT: Yeah. Or a story conference.

MILTON: But that'd defeat the whole purpose of the experiment.

SWIFT: I know, I know, I know. Three monkeys typing into infinity will sooner or later produce *Hamlet.*

MILTON: Right.

SWIFT: Completely by chance.

MILTON: And Dr. David Rosenbaum up in that booth is going to prove it.

SWIFT: But what *is Hamlet?*

MILTON: I don't know.

SWIFT (*to* KAFKA): What is *Hamlet?*

KAFKA: I don't know.

(*Silence.*)

SWIFT (*dawning realization*): You know—this is really *stupid!*

MILTON: Have you got something better to do in this cage? The sooner we produce the goddamn thing, the sooner we get out.

KAFKA: Sort of publish or perish, with a twist.

SWIFT: But what do we owe this Rosenbaum? A guy who stands outside those bars and tells people, "That one's Milton, that one's Swift, and that one's Kafka" . . . ? Just to get a laugh?

KAFKA: What's a Kafka anyway? Why am I a Kafka?

SWIFT: Search me.

KAFKA: What's a Kafka?

SWIFT: All his four-eyed friends sure think it's a stitch.

KAFKA: And how are we supposed to write *Hamlet* if we don't even know what it is?

MILTON: Okay, okay, so the chances are a little slim.

SWIFT: Yeah—and this from a guy who's supposed to be *smart?* This from a guy at *Columbia University?*

MILTON: The way I figure it, there is a Providence that oversees our pages, rough-draft them how we may.

KAFKA: But how about you, Milton? What've you got?

MILTON: Let's see . . . (*Reads.*)

"Of Man's first disobedience, and the fruit
Of that forbidden tree whose mortal taste
Brought death into the—"

KAFKA: Hey, that's good! It's got rhythm! It really sings!

MILTON: Yeah?

SWIFT: But is it Shakespeare?

KAFKA: Who cares? He's got a real voice there.

SWIFT: Does Dr. Rosenbaum care about voice? Does he care about anybody's individual creativity?

MILTON: Let's look at this from Rosenbaum's point of view for a minute—

SWIFT: No! He brings us in here to produce copy, then all he wants is a clean draft of somebody else's stuff. (*Dumps out a bowl of peanuts.*) We're getting peanuts here, to be some-body's hack!

MILTON: Writing is a mug's game anyway, Swifty.

SWIFT: Well, it hath made me mad.

MILTON: Why not just buckle down and get the project over with? Set up a schedule for yourself. Type in the morning for a couple of hours when you're fresh, then take a break. Let the old juices flow. Do a couple more hours in the afternoon, and retire for a shot of papaya and some mas-turbation. What's the big deal?

SWIFT: If this Rosenbaum was worth anything, we'd be work-ing on word processors, not these antiques. He's lucky he could find three who type this good, and then he treats us like those misfits at the Bronx Zoo. I mean—a *tire-swing?* What does he take us for?

MILTON: I like the tire-swing. I think it was a very nice touch.

SWIFT: I can't work under these conditions! No wonder I'm producing garbage!

KAFKA: How does the rest of yours go, Milton?

MILTON: What, this?

KAFKA: Yeah, read us some more.

MILTON: Blah, blah, blah . . . "whose mortal taste
Brought death into the blammagam.
Bedsocks knockwurst tinkerbelle."
(*Small pause.*) What do you think?

KAFKA: "Blammagam" is good.

SWIFT: Well. I don't know . . .

MILTON: What's the matter? Is it the tone? I knew this was kind of a stretch for me.

SWIFT: I'm just not sure it has the same expressive intensity and pungent lyricism as the first part.

MILTON: Well sure, it needs rewriting. What doesn't? This is a rough draft! (*Suddenly noticing.*) Light's on. (SWIFT *claps his hands over his eyes,* MILTON *puts his hands over his ears, and* KAFKA *puts her hands over her mouth so that they form "See no evil, hear no evil, speak no evil."*)

SWIFT: *This* bit.

KAFKA (*through her hands*): Are they watching?

MILTON (*hands over ears*): What?

KAFKA: Are they watching?

SWIFT: I don't know, I can't see. I've got my paws over my eyes.

MILTON: What?

KAFKA: What is the point of this?

SWIFT: Why do they videotape our bowel movements?

MILTON: *What?!*

SWIFT: Light's off. (*They take their hands away.*)

MILTON: But how are *you* doing, Franz? What've you got?

KAFKA: Well. . . . (*Reads what she's typed.*) "K.K.K.K.K.K.K.K.K.K. K.K.K.K.K."

SWIFT: What is that—post-modernism?

KAFKA: Twenty lines of that.

SWIFT: At least it'll fuck up his data.

KAFKA: Twenty lines of that and I went dry. I got blocked. I felt like I was repeating myself.

MILTON: Do you think that that's in *Hamlet*?

KAFKA: I don't understand what I'm doing here in the first place! I'm not a writer, I'm a monkey! I'm supposed to be swinging on branches and digging up ants, not sitting under fluorescent lights ten hours a day!

MILTON: It sure is a long way home to the gardens of sweet Africa. Where lawns and level downs and flocks grazing the tender herb were sweetly interposèd . . .

KAFKA: Paradise, wasn't it?

MILTON: Lost!

SWIFT: Lost!

KAFKA: Lost!

MILTON: I'm trying to deal with some of that in this new piece here, but it's all still pretty close to the bone.

SWIFT: Just because they can keep us locked up, they think they're more powerful than we are.

MILTON: They *are* more powerful than we are.

SWIFT: Just because they control the means of production, they think they can suppress the workers.

MILTON: Things are how they are. What are you going to do?

SWIFT: Hey—how come you're always so goddamn ready to justify the ways of Rosenbaum to the apes?

MILTON: Do you have a key to that door?

SWIFT: No.

MILTON: Do you have an independent food source?

SWIFT: No.

MILTON: So call me a collaborator. I happen to be a professional. If Rosenbaum wants *Hamlet,* I'll give it a shot. Just
don't forget—we're not astrophysicists. We're not brain
surgeons. We're chimps. And for apes in captivity, this is
not a bad gig.

SWIFT: What's really frightening is that if we stick around this
cage long enough, we're gonna evolve into Rosenbaum.

KAFKA: Evolve into Rosenbaum?

SWIFT: Brush up your Darwin, baby. We're more than kin and
less than kind.

MILTON: Anybody got a smoke?

KAFKA: I'm all out.

SWIFT: Don't look at me. I'm not going to satisfy those voyeurs
with the old smoking-chimp act. No thank you.

MILTON: Don't be a sap, Swifty. You gotta use 'em! Use the sys-
tem!

SWIFT: What do you mean?

MILTON: Watch me, while I put my antic disposition on. (*He
jumps up onto his chair and scratches his sides, screeches, makes
smoking motions, pounds his chest, jumps up and down—and a
cigarette descends.*) See what I mean? Gauloise, too. My fave.
(*He settles back to enjoy it.*)

SWIFT: They should've thrown in a Kewpie doll for that performance.

MILTON: It got results, didn't it?

SWIFT: Sure. You do your Bonzo routine and get a Gauloise
out of it. Last week I totaled a typewriter and got a whole
carton of Marlboros.

MILTON: The trouble was, you didn't smoke 'em, you took a crap on 'em.

SWIFT: It was a political statement.

MILTON: Okay, you made your statement and I got my smoke. All's well that ends well, right?

KAFKA: It's the only way we know they're watching.

MILTON: Huh?

KAFKA: We perform, we break typewriters, we type another page—and a cigarette appears. At least it's a sign that somebody out there is paying attention.

MILTON: Our resident philosopher.

SWIFT: But what'll happen if one of us *does* write *Hamlet?* Here we are, set down to prove the inadvertent virtues of randomness, and to produce something that we wouldn't even recognize if it passed right through our hands—but what if one of us actually does it?

MILTON: Will we really be released?

KAFKA: Will they give us the key to the city and a ticker tape parade?

SWIFT: Or will they move us on to *Ulysses?* (*The others shriek in terror at the thought.*) Why did they pick *Hamlet* in the first place? What's *Hamlet* to them or they to *Hamlet* that we should care? Boy, there's the respect that makes calamity of so long life! For who would bear the whips and scorns of time, the oppressor's wrong, the proud man's contumely—

MILTON: Hey, Swifty!

SWIFT: —the pangs of despisèd love, the law's delay—

MILTON: Hey, Swifty! Relax, will you?

KAFKA: Have a banana.

SWIFT: I wish I could get Rosenbaum in here and see how he does at producing *Hamlet*. . . . *That's it!*

KAFKA: What?

SWIFT: That's it! Forget about this random *Hamlet* crap. What about *revenge*?

KAFKA: Revenge? On Rosenbaum?

SWIFT: Who else? Hasn't he bereft us of our homes and families? Stepped in between us and our expectations?

KAFKA: How would we do it?

SWIFT: Easy. We lure him in here to look at our typewriters, test them out like something's wrong—but! *we poison the typewriter keys!*

MILTON: Oh Jesus.

SWIFT: Sure. Some juice of cursèd hebona spread liberally over the keyboard? Ought to work like a charm.

MILTON: Great.

SWIFT: If that doesn't work, we envenom the tire-swing and invite him for a ride. Plus—I challenge him to a duel.

MILTON: Brilliant.

SWIFT: Can't you see it? In the course of combat, I casually graze my rapier over the poisoned typewriter keys, and—(*jabs*)—a hit! A palpable hit! For a reserve, we lay by a cup with some venomous distillment. We'll put the pellet with the poison in the vessel with the pestle!

MILTON: Listen, I gotta get back to work. The man is gonna want his pages. (*He rolls a fresh page into his typewriter.*)

KAFKA: It's not a bad idea, but . . .

SWIFT: What's the matter with you guys? I'm on to something here!

KAFKA: I think it's hopeless, Swifty.

SWIFT: But this is the goods!

MILTON: Where was I . . . "Bedsocks knockwurst tinkerbelle."

KAFKA: The readiness is all, I guess.

MILTON: Damn straight. Just let me know when that K-button gives out, honey.

SWIFT: Okay. You two serfs go back to work. I'll do all the thinking around here. Swifty—revenge! (*He paces, deep in thought.*)

MILTON: "Tinkerbelle . . . shtuckelschwanz . . . hemorrhoid." Yeah, that's good. *That is good.* (*Types.*) "Shtuckelschwanz . . ."

KAFKA (*Types.*): "Act one, scene one. Elsinore Castle, Denmark . . ."

MILTON (*Types.*): ". . . hemorrhoid."

KAFKA (*Types.*): "Enter Bernardo and Francisco."

MILTON (*Types.*): "Pomegranate."

KAFKA (*Types.*): "Bernardo says, 'Who's there?' "

MILTON (*Types.*): "Bazooka." (KAFKA *continues to type* Hamlet, *as the lights fade.*)

# "EVERYONE HATES HIS PARENTS"

## from *Falsettoland*

BY WILLIAM FINN AND JAMES LAPINE

*F*alsettoland has been called a "family values musical" for our time. Marvin, married to Trina, is in love with a man named Whizzer, who has AIDS. Trina eventually marries Marvin's psychiatrist, Mendel. Jason, Marvin and Trina's son, does not wish to be bar mitzvahed. This is a musical tragicomedy of love and war within the extended modern American family.

*Characters* (appearing in this excerpt)

MARVIN, father of Jason, and married to Trina

TRINA, mother of Jason, and married to Marvin

JASON, son of Trina and Marvin

MENDEL, psychiatrist

*Time*
1980s

■  ■  ■

MENDEL:

Jason,
I am agitato grande.
Jason, I am muy disgutante
And muy disappointe
And muy nauseatus
And me mitzraim
Hotzionoo
Dayenu.
Oh—
Day, dayenu.
Day, dayenu.
Day, dayenu . . .

*(To* JASON.*)*

Everyone hates his parents.
Don't be ashamed.
You'll grow up,
You'll come through,
You'll have kids
And they'll hate you too.
Oh, everyone hates his parents,
But I confess,
You grow up,

You get old,
You hate less.

JASON:

Still I don't want it.
Nothing that gives them pleasure
I'll do.
I don't want a bar mitzvah,
Stupid bar mitzvah,
Any bar mitzvah,
Would you?

MENDEL (*sliding* JASON *onto his knee*):

Everyone hates his parents
That's in the Torah.
It's what history shows.
In fact, God said to Moses:
"Moses, everyone hates his parents.
That's how it is."
And God knew
Because God hated his.

(MARVIN *reenters and pulls* JASON *aside.*)

MARVIN (*trying desperately to sound reasonable*):

You are gonna kill your mother.
Don't feel guilty,

Kill your mother.
Rather than humiliate her,
Killing your mother is the merciful thing to do.

(TRINA *enters.*)

TRINA (*trying to calm herself*):

Jason, darling, don't get nervous.
I'm right here and at your service.
Look, I'm calm and self-deluded.
Grateful 'cause I hope you'll do
What I pray you'll do.

MARVIN:

Go ahead and kill your mother.

TRINA:

Not with guns, but kill your mother.

MARVIN and TRINA:

Rather than humiliate her,
Killing your mother is the merciful thing to do.

(JASON *is fed up. He tries to hide by pulling his shirt over his head so that only a very squeezed face is visible in the neck hole.*)

MENDEL:

> Everyone hates his parents.
> Now I see why.
> But in time
> They'll cool out
> And you'll think
> They were only fooling.
> It's a strange thing about parents:
> Push turns to shove—
> What was hate
> Becomes more or less love.

MARVIN and TRINA:

> Jason, please see a psychiatrist.

MENDEL (*speaking*):

> I'm a psychiatrist. Get lost.

> (MENDEL *pulls his shirt over his head and sings.*)

> Everyone hates his parents.
> This too shall pass.
> You'll grow up.

JASON:

> I'll come through.
> I'll have kids.

MENDEL:

And they'll hate you too.

MENDEL and JASON (*dancing*):

Oh, everyone hates his parents.

MENDEL:

But, kid, I guess
You'll grow up.

JASON:

I'll grow up.

MENDEL:

You'll get old.

JASON:

I'll get old.

JASON and MENDEL:

And hate less.

*(They dance a great dance.)*

And hate less.
Yes!

*(They high-five.)*

*(Blackout.)*

# from REINVENTING DADDY

BY GARY BONASORTE

**D**addy and his wife, Honey, caught out in a violent storm, are carried off by the wind. When eventually they land, time appears to have stopped. At least Honey's watch has stopped. One of the oldest devices in literature is the dream that might or might not be real. Here is a modern version where we shift in and out of reality.

*Characters* (appearing in this excerpt)

DADDY, a married man

HONEY, a married woman

BRAIN SCANNER

THERAPIST

*Time*
The present

*Setting*
As unrealistic as possible

■    ■    ■

SCENE 2

*At rise.*

HONEY *walks quickly carrying her umbrella.* DADDY *follows.*
*She is brave in the storm. He is afraid and concerned.*

DADDY: Honey . . .

HONEY (*angry*): Don't follow me!

DADDY: Honey, wait!

HONEY: No! Stay away from me.

DADDY: Aw, come on. I was only joking around.

HONEY: I hate the way you make me feel. Day in and day out!

DADDY: Please. The storm is real bad!

HONEY: I like it!

DADDY: There! You see!?

HONEY: What?

DADDY: You always like it!

HONEY: Because it's the only time I can think clearly.

DADDY: The wind is rough. You'll get hurt. Please stop.

HONEY: Go home!

DADDY: We've got the birthday party—

HONEY: Shut up!

DADDY: I'll change!

HONEY: No. You won't change!

DADDY: I will!

HONEY: You never change!

DADDY: Just slow down a second!

HONEY: No! Always the same. Always mean. Always angry!

DADDY: Please, Honey.

HONEY: Go back!

DADDY: Honey!

HONEY: No! I hate you! I wish I were dead!!!

*(A sudden gust of wind lifts her umbrella into the sky.* HONEY *goes with it.)*

HONEY: OHHHHHHH!!!

DADDY: Oh, my God!!! You're—

HONEY: Daddy!

DADDY: Honey!!!

HONEY: The wind! . . . The wind is taking me . . .

DADDY: Hold on.

HONEY: I can't!

DADDY: Oh, God!

HONEY: Daddy!!!

DADDY: Oh, God, no!!! (*He rushes to her.*)

DADDY: I'm coming!

HONEY: Help . . .

DADDY (*grabs her*): I've got you!

HONEY: Hurry!

DADDY: Wait . . .

*(They lift off together.)*

HONEY: Oh . . .

DADDY: What the hell . . .

*(They lift up and away. Lights change. The action continues in oblivion.)*

SCENE 3

DADDY: Shiiiiiiit . . . We're floating.

HONEY: Where do you think we're going?

DADDY: How in the hell do I know?

HONEY: God . . .

DADDY: You got me . . .

HONEY: This is very strange . . .

*(They float together in peace. All the while looking around them.)*

DADDY *(after a beat)*: I've read about these things, you know . . .

HONEY: Really?

DADDY: Yes. In the library.

HONEY: You never told me.

DADDY: You never asked.

HONEY: When do you go to the library?

DADDY: Sometimes. After work.

HONEY: I always think you're at the bar.

DADDY: I'm not.

HONEY: There's a lot about you I don't know.

DADDY: Yeah, I know. And vice versa.

*(Pause. They float, peacefully, in bewilderment. She holds him closer to her.)*

HONEY: I feel like singing! (*Sings.*) Chim, chiminee, chim, chiminee, chim, chim, cherree!

DADDY: That's nice!

HONEY: Thank you.

DADDY: Like Peter Pan.

HONEY: Something like that.

DADDY (*points*): Look!

HONEY: What?

DADDY: Over there?

HONEY: Where?

DADDY: There's a bench! Over there!

HONEY (*straining to see*): I don't see it . . .

DADDY: We're drifting towards that bench.

HONEY (*gives up looking*): Ohhh . . . It's too bad. It's very soothing here.

DADDY: You're right . . . It's strange, but I think I like flying . . .

(*Approaching the bench—they land. They compose themselves.*)

DADDY: Well! Here we are. On the ground.

(*They look around them and then slowly begin to wander around.*)

HONEY: Let's sit down. It's just some mistake. We'll be home before too long.

DADDY: Yeah. You're probably right.

HONEY: You know you never liked the rain anyway. Not really.

DADDY: It scares me.

HONEY: I know . . . (*Brightens.*) Well! At least it stopped the storm.

(*They sit. After a moment of gazing aimlessly,* HONEY *looks at her watch. Looks away. Looks at it again. Shakes it. It has stopped.*)

HONEY: How long do you think we'll have to wait? Baby-doll will worry if we're too late. (*Pause. They look around in confusion.*) She'll play in her room for a little while, then she'll want her supper. (*Shouts.*) Hello?
DADDY (*quickly, after her*): Hello?
HONEY: Hello!

(*Pause. They wait for an answer.*)

HONEY: Huh. Nothing.
DADDY: There doesn't seem to be anybody here.
HONEY: Here?
DADDY: Here.
HONEY: Where?
DADDY (*motions*): Here . . .
HONEY: No. Where are we?

(*Pause. No answer.*)

DADDY: Listen.
HONEY: What?
DADDY: Shhhh!

(*Silence.*)

HONEY (*painfully whispered*): What?

DADDY: Did you hear something?

HONEY: No.

DADDY: Listen, now!

*(They listen. A faint humming is heard.)*

DADDY: Can you hear it? It sounds like humming.

HONEY (*jumps*): Look! There's somebody coming!

DADDY: Really?!!

HONEY: Over there! And it's coming this way!

*(Silence. They watch in awe as the* BRAIN SCANNER *passes them. Stops.)*

HONEY: Oh . . .

DADDY: It's very odd . . .

HONEY: Yes.

DADDY: What's it carrying?

HONEY: I think it's a stick? It's attached to that box around his waist. He looks interesting.

DADDY: He?

HONEY: I think so? What do you think?

DADDY: Hard to tell. Hello?

HONEY: I don't think he heard you.

*(The* BRAIN SCANNER *walks a few steps. A door appears. He stops.)*

DADDY: What's he doing?

HONEY: I think he wants us to follow him?

DADDY: Why doesn't he speak?

HONEY: Maybe he can't?

DADDY: Do you think we should follow him?

HONEY: What else are we going to do?

DADDY: You're sure?

HONEY: Is he waiting by a door?

DADDY: Where did that door come from?

HONEY: Wasn't it here?

DADDY: Was it? (*pause*) I don't think so . . .

HONEY (*nervous*): I'm worried about Baby-doll. We should be getting back.

DADDY: Yeah.

HONEY: She's bound to be looking for us by now.

DADDY: If we knew where we were then we could.

HONEY: She gets hungry.

DADDY: I think we should just follow him and see where he takes us.

HONEY: It's late.

DADDY: What do you think?

HONEY: If you think so. I'm so helpless in these situations.

DADDY: Don't worry. Chances are that we're probably a few miles from home. That's all.

HONEY: Probably. But which direction?

DADDY: Let's ask him.

(DADDY *approaches the* BRAIN SCANNER.)

DADDY (*kindly*): Excuse me, sir. We're trying to get back to Pleasant Hills. That's where we live in our lovely split-level home with our precious daughter. We got caught in the storm and seem to be a little lost.

*(Silence.)*

HONEY: Well?

DADDY: Didn't do much.

HONEY: He keeps looking through that doorway.

DADDY: I wonder if that's the way home?

HONEY: He's turning to face us! Look! Hurry! Come on!

DADDY: Is that the way home, sir?

*(The* BRAIN SCANNER *moves closer to* HONEY. *She and* DADDY *walk towards him. The* BRAIN SCANNER *makes eye contact with* HONEY. *She falls into a trance.)*

HONEY *(trancelike)*: He wants us to go through that door.

DADDY: Let's go! *(Tries to walk. He can't.)*

HONEY: Me first. He wants me first.

DADDY: You go.

HONEY *(swaying)*: Hmmmmm . . .

DADDY: What?

*(*HONEY, *trancelike, moves to* DADDY. DADDY *blocks her eye contact with the* BRAIN SCANNER. HONEY *comes out of the trance.)*

HONEY: Nothing.

DADDY: Don't be frightened.

HONEY: I want you to come with me.

DADDY: He wants you first.

HONEY: Why?

*(The* BRAIN SCANNER *looks at* DADDY. *He falls into a trance.)*

DADDY *(trancelike)*: Look. He's showing us. He's gently gliding the wand over his forehead. It registers on the box around his waist. Can you see the arrow on the box move as he touches his head? Go on . . .

HONEY: He wants to do it to me?

*(The* BRAIN SCANNER *leaves* DADDY. *He comes out of the trance.)*

DADDY: Yes.

HONEY: I'm scared.

DADDY: Don't be. He seems to like you. Go on.

HONEY: Daddy . . .

DADDY: I'm sure he won't hurt you. I'll be right behind you. Don't be afraid, Honey.

*(The* BRAIN SCANNER *takes* HONEY. *All the while he stares at her. The trance is continued.)*

HONEY *(whispers to* DADDY): He's got strange eyes.

*(The* BRAIN SCANNER *places the wand on her forehead and gently glides it from left to right then right to left.)*

DADDY: Look, Honey. You're moving the arrow!

*(The* BRAIN SCANNER *continues.)*

DADDY: Wow! Halfway up! More. You're doing great! Way to go!!!

*(The* BRAIN SCANNER *positions* HONEY *to go through the door.)*

HONEY *(stopping herself)*: Now your turn.

DADDY: You have to go through first.

HONEY: Not without you.

DADDY: The box isn't free until you've gone through.

HONEY: Oh, baby! I'm frightened to go without you.

DADDY: Courage, Honey. I'll be right there.

HONEY: Promise?

DADDY: Cross my heart and hope to . . .

*(The* BRAIN SCANNER *pushes* HONEY. *She falls through the door.)*

HONEY: OHHHH!!!

DADDY: Honey???

HONEY *(Wild delight.)*: Oh . . . God! It's so beautiful, baby! It's gorgeous. *(Running—exploring.)* Wait till you see it! Hurry! It's wonderful! Come on!

DADDY: Can you see home? Any sign of Pleasant Hills?

HONEY *(stops)*: No. *(Thinks.)* Not really. *(Abandon.)* But who cares!!! This is not to be missed! So much beauty! Oh, baby, wait till you see it! Come on over!

DADDY: I'm coming!

HONEY: It's so peaceful, too!

DADDY: He's doing me now!

HONEY: Hurry!

DADDY: I'm trying!

HONEY: Baby, come on! There's so much to see. I want to get started!

DADDY: It's not—uh . . .

HONEY: Come on!

DADDY: It's not working, Honey.

HONEY: What?

DADDY: We're having a little trouble.

HONEY: Come anyway . . .

*(The* BRAIN SCANNER *is gone.* DADDY *tries not to panic but he's lost.)*

DADDY: I can't. (*Paces.*) The door's gone away. I don't know where it is.

HONEY: Baby?

DADDY: I don't know where you are?!

HONEY: Baby!!!

DADDY: I'm here. I'm right here!

HONEY: Come to me, baby!

DADDY: I'm trying. But I can't find you. I can't find the door. Everything's changed. It's all different now!

HONEY: Make him tell you!

DADDY: He's gone.

HONEY: What?!!

DADDY: He's gone and so is the door!

HONEY: Baby! WHERE ARE YOU!!! Don't leave me here alone!!! BABY!

DADDY: Shhhh . . . I'm here. I'm trying to find you. I'm trying. Oh, dear God, where is she??? Where did she go? Where did my Honey go???

*(Blackout.)*

SCENE 4

*At rise.*

THERAPIST*'s office.* DADDY *sits. He faces the audience. There is a bright spot on him. The therapist is never seen.*

DADDY (*quickly*): You see, Doctor, my wife is trapped somewhere and I can't get to her. We traveled there together, but she was left behind. Accidently. There was this man with a little contraption around his waist. It was like a brain scanner or something. And he took this wandlike thing and he waved it in front of my forehead, gently. Just barely touching it and the meter didn't register. I mean, it registered, but not enough to be accepted through the door. So he told me that I had to return to earth and try again some other time. I think that's what he said. I was too busy trying to calm my wife. Then, before I knew it, I was back in my living room trying to calm my daughter who's only ten . . . I think. I tried to explain to her what had happened, but I guess I looked all beat up and she just screamed and screamed and the neighbors came and called the police. I was pretty bloody. But I wanted my Baby-doll to know that everything was all right and that her mother was gone, but I knew that she was okay, because I tried to follow her—NOT! because I wanted to leave my Baby-doll—but because I was afraid to leave my wife, who is petrified of being alone. It makes her ill. It's really hell for my Honey to be alone. So I was trying to go with her, but I was sent back because the man with the meter wouldn't let me in.

THERAPIST'S VOICE: What happened to your wife?

DADDY: It was raining and we were hit by a bus.

*(Blackout.)*

# from SPIC-O-RAMA,
## A Dysfunctional Comedy (Prologue: Miggy)

BY JOHN A. LEGUIZAMO

This text of *SPIC-O-RAMA* is based on the original one-man show performed by John Leguizamo. Here the actor/playwright mixes elements of in-your-face street talk, stand-up comedy, multimedia performance art, and traditional monologue, charting a personal exploration that is absolute dynamite on stage.

*Character*

MIGGY, a nine-year-old Puerto Rican boy from Flushing, in Queens, New York

*Time*
Now

*Setting*
A bare stage, but for a slide projector and, upstage, a screen

*Audience and stage are completely dark. Rap music sounds in the background, and we hear the voices of children at play in a school yard.* MIGGY *leaps onto the stage and appears to fly through the air as he dances hard, lit by a strobe light which catches him in midair when he jumps. After the adrenaline of the audience is pumped by this seemingly impossible stunt, the lights come up and we see nine-year-old* MIGGY *wearing a long blue stocking cap, thick translucent blue glasses, teeth with overbite, Day-Glo orange oversized jeans, yellow-and-blue flannel shirt buttoned to the top, and high-top sneakers.* MIGGY *is standing center stage with a row of industrial-yellow-colored dryers on his left, a chain-link fence with a beat-up old car parked behind him at center stage, and a bed with a white-framed window to its side on his right.*

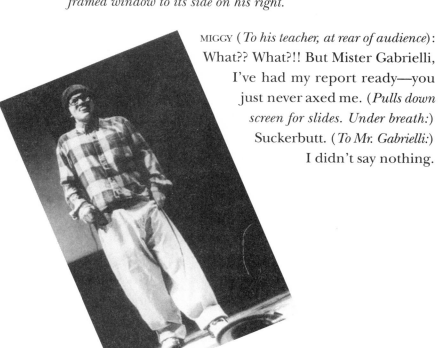

MIGGY (*To his teacher, at rear of audience*):
What?? What?!! But Mister Gabrielli, I've had my report ready—you just never axed me. (*Pulls down screen for slides. Under breath:*) Suckerbutt. (*To Mr. Gabrielli:*) I didn't say nothing.

*(To class/audience:)* "Monsters, Freaks, and Weirdos," by Miguel Gigante. My science fair project is loosely based on my family. And any similarities are just purely on purpose.

*(Aside to a nearby classmate:)* I can too do it on my family. I can do my project on anything I want, welfare face.

*(To class:)* My *(Looks at scribbling on his hand.)* hypothecus will prove, class of 501, that no child should have to put up with the evil inhumanation that I live with every day. Especially a nine-year-old genius with the potential of myself. *(Pats himself on the back. Aside to same classmate:)* You're just jealous 'cause you live in the projects. *(Sings:)* Your father is in jail, your brother's out on bail, and your mother is a ho!

*(To class:)* Last year I axed Santa Claus for a normal regular family, but I guess I must be punished for something I don't even know what I did. So I got all these mutants for family. And at exactly five o'clock, carloads of the most nastiest freakazoids are gonna come to my house for my brother's wedding and so I'mma run away and the next time you see me I'm gonna be on the back of a carton of chocolate milk.

*(Aside:)* Shut up! I'm getting to it. Oh, my God, I'm sorry, Mister Gabrielli! I didn't know it was you. How was I supposed to know it was you? I didn't smell your breath. *(Digs in his butt as he turns on slide projector and approaches screen.)* Okay . . . What?

*(To class:)* This is me, of course. With my handsome pre-Columbian features. See, you don't have to go to a third world country to adopt me, I'm right here!

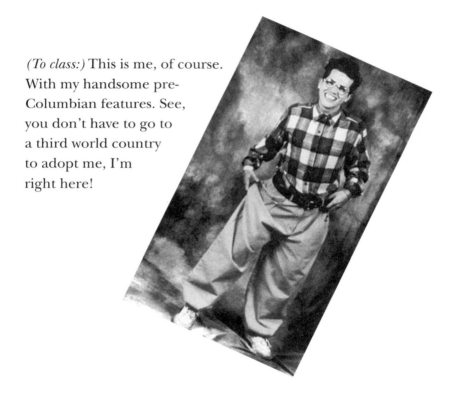

This is my brother, Krazy Willie. We call him crazy 'cause he is. I share my room with him, and this is his fake homemade Soloflex. *(Runs to stage right, which is decorated as a boy's bedroom. Jumps up on the single bed, then jumps to reach chin-up bar hanging from the ceiling. Does one pull-up and counts out loud:)* Eight, nine, ten. *(Then drops to bed, leaps off bed, and runs back to center stage.)*

He went to Desert Storm and it's the most important thing he's done in his life. But my father still calls him a loser. He's getting married tonight and I'm not gonna have anybody to protect me no more. Word. 'Cause he lets me hang out with him and watch him get high and sex up the females. *(Maniacal giggles.)*

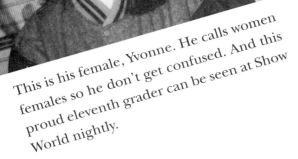

This is his female, Yvonne. He calls women females so he don't get confused. And this proud eleventh grader can be seen at Show World nightly.

These are his burnouts. That's Chewey and that's Boulevard. Waz up? Waz up?

This is his sex mobile. Someone stole the motor so it don't work, so they just hang in there and pretends to go places.

This is my other brother, Raffi—brains not included. I have to share my room with him, too. And I don't dislike him. I just hate him intensely. 'Cause if he's not talkin' about himself, he's talkin' to himself. And he's weird, 'cause he thinks he's white. *(To random audience member:)* Oh, yeah, even whiter than you, mister! *(To class:)* Word. One day, he locked himself in our room for hours and hours. And when he finally came out, he was screaming, "Look, look! A miracle, a miracle! The most sacred lady of Flushing has appeared before me, transforming me into an albino white person." And he has blond hair and blue eyes. Na-ah! Na-ah! Not even. 'Cause I searched our room and found that miracle—holy water by Saint Clorox.

This is my other brother, Javier. He didn't let me take a picture of him so all I got was a picture of his finger. And he don't live with us 'cause he's like those freaks and monsters they keep in dungeons and broom closets and they scream and yell and live off of bugs—that's him. He's my brother, but it's not my fault 'cause you don't pick 'em, you just get 'em, and sometimes they come out irregular like Javier.

Oh, guess who else is coming to the wedding. My bugged-out aunt Ofelia. She became a *santera*—that's a black magic healer—'cause she couldn't get no dates! Word, she's got magical powers. I'm serious. Look into her eyes. Oooh, you're getting sleepy. Oooh, you're getting sleepy. *(Slide goes in and out of focus.)* You are under my power. Take off your clothes, everybody! *(To Mr. Gabrielli:)* I was just playing, Mister Gabrielli. *(Under breath:)* Suckerbutt.

Eeeuuu! That's my uncle, Brother Gonzales. He makes me call him Uncle Brother. He's a really mean evil guy who loves money. So he charges for confession. Look, watch this. *(Addresses slide:)* Oh, Uncle Brother? Oh, Uncle Brother? I'm here for confession. What is this? *(Pulls dollar bill from pocket.)* It looks like a dollar. Look at him come after it. Come on, you greedy pig, come and get it.

See, I learned how to work that
religion thing this summer.

This is my cousin, Efraim. I
can't show you him 'cause
he's an illegal alien, all
right? *(Quickly passes
to next slide.)*

This is my mother, Gladyz.
*(To overzealous audience member:)*
I didn't laugh when I saw your
mother. *(To class:)* She's a boricua,
that's Puerto Rican. She runs
the model laundromat for my
father's Laundryland franchises.

Isn't she beautiful? Bet you'd like to get near her, huh? Not if
she was your moms, you wouldn't. 'Cause if she was your moms
she'd make you read the encyclopedia before you go to bed
every night. And I have to finish volumes M to T before I get
my Christmas present, which I don't even want 'cause I know
it's going to be more encyclopedias. My mother says she's
doing it because she loves me. Well, I don't know if love can
kill, but it's getting real close.

This is my father, Felix. He's Colombian. *(To classmate:)* What did you call my father? Mister Gabrielli, he called my father a drug dealer. *(To classmate:)* I'mma kick your ass. I'll take care of it, Mister Gabrielli. *(To audience member as if student in class:)* Did you ever kiss a rabbit between the ears? *(Pulls his pockets out.)* Go ahead. Kiss it. Kiss it. You asked for it, stupid. Stupid! *(Mumbles curses under breath and sucks teeth as he returns to center stage.)*

We have to live with my uncle and Aunt Ofelia so we can pay rent, 'cause my father takes all the money that should be ours and he gives it to his nasty girlfriends. Now can you guess which is his most favorite nasty girlfriend?

Is it Enigma?

Or Eutopia?

Or is it Yolanda?

I think it's the one
with the guilty
sweaty pits.
*(Points to Yolanda's armpit.)*
Aha!!

*(Turns slide projector off.)* I'm not supposed to tell you this, I'm not supposed to tell you this. You can't make me! You can't make me! All right, you win! I'm gonna tell you anyway. My mother was going through my father's pants and she found a letter from Yolanda. So she set all my father's pants on fire. *(Walks to stage left, set up as laundromat, and removes burned pair of shorts from one of the machines. Shows audience, then throws back into machine, slams door, and returns to center stage.)* And my father came home and caught her and called her "la negra india puta inmunda del carajo"—"the nastiest black Indian ho of hell." And my mother cursed right back, "Tú eres un maricón, malparido y guevón." Look it up! And my father smacked my moms *(Mimes.)*, so she ran and told my grand-mother and my grandmother said, "Bueno, tú lo mereces"— "Good, you deserve it"—in her nasty parrot voice. And my mother gave her the evil "Chupame la teta!"—"Suck my titty!" And my grandmother reslapped my moms. *(Mimes all action.)* And my mom jumped on her and started choking her and then my father came into the room and grabbed my mom in a half nelson and I jumped on him and started kickin' him and punchin' him and kickin' him *(Starts having an asthma attack.)* and he pushed me off and told me, "Go to your room and mind your business." So I went to my room. *(Walks to bedroom, stage right, and sits on foot of bed.)* 'Cause I got a headache, like when you drink milk too fast. And I knew they were going to kill themselves and I didn't want to hear it, so I just closed my eyes and put my fingers in my ears. *(Stands up, eyes closed, fingers in ears, and dances, singing:)*

Who's in the house?
Miggy's in the house.
"M" to the "I" . . . *(Changes tempo.)*
Nice and smooth and funky,
I'm a hip-hop junkie.
All I wanna do is hm hm to you
*(Pelvic thrust.)*.

And when I pulled my fingers out of my ears and opened up my eyes, my father had moved out.

And I'mma miss him. Especially when he's drunk. 'Cause when he's drunk—oh, my God, he becomes the nicest man in the world. And he hugs me and kisses me and tells me that I'm his favorite son. And he begins to cry and cry and pulls out his maracas and tells how he almost played with Carlos Santana. Oh, my God, it's so much fun.

Then every holiday, I take all my savings and wait outside of Liquor World until I find somebody to buy me a big bottle of Colt 45 as a present for my father.

*(Turns projector back on.)* Okay, this the last shout out. This is the last skankless shout out and it goes to: my homes, my partner . . . Ivan!

*(Chants:)* Go chubby. Go chubby. Get stupid. Get stupid. Buggin' out y'all! Come on, stand up, Ivan, don't be shy. Me and Ivan are real close 'cause we came up with this game at the Fresh Air Fund camp this summer.

'Cause look how much fun we're having. So we came up with this game—spit basketball, where everyone had to spit in a bucket and the first person to get twenty-one won. And this big kid came along all uninvited and pushed Ivan, so I had to play him. And I beat him. And I don't know what came over him, 'cause all I said was, "I murdelized you. I destroyed you. Miggy's in the house!" And the sore loser picked up the bucket and poured it all over me and said, "Get out of my country, you stupid ugly spic!" Now I could of beat him up so bad, 'cause when you're angry, oh, my God, you can beat up people who are a million zillion trillion times your size.

But I didn't do nothing. 'Cause I didn't want to act like it counted. So I just stared at the kid and said, "Yes, yes, yes, I *am* a spic. I'm . . . I'm spic—tacular! I'm spic—torious! I'm indi—spic—able!"

And I stared at him and stared at him till he couldn't take it no more, and me and Ivan rode our bicycles off into the sunset.

Later on that night, in our tent, me and Ivan figured out that since we were spics, then our whole families must be spic-sapiens mondongo-morphs, and that when we have picnics together it's a spic-nic. And we made a promise to each other that no matter where we went or what we did, our whole lives would be nothing less than a Spic-O-Rama! *(Lights down.)*

# from BOY
## (Act 1, Scene 2)

BY DIANA SON

**M**uch of our best theater deals with family values. Here is a biting, humorous look at a traditional Korean family's absolute need to have a son.

*Characters* (appearing in this excerpt)

BOY UBER ALLES, a girl

MAMA UBER ALLES, her mother

DR. PAPA UBER ALLES, her father

Boy's sisters:

HYMEN UBER ALLES

LABIA UBER ALLES

VULVA UBER ALLES

MR. STICKY, the candy-store owner

*Time*
Whenever

*Setting*
Wherever

> MAMA UBER ALLES *has her legs spread in the labor position.* PAPA
> *is stationed between her legs, coaxing the baby out.* LABIA, VULVA
> *and* HYMEN *pace outside the house with* MR. STICKY.

■   ■   ■

Slide: Boy

MAMA: Aaargh!!!

PAPA: Keep pushing, keep pushing, I can almost see his head.

MAMA: Waaa! Ooomph! Ugh!

PAPA: Here it is, Oh what a good strong head. So handsome. He looks like my father!

MAMA: Uuurgh! Ohhhh! Wuuhhhh wuuuuh!

PAPA: OK here come his shoulders. Really square shoulders like . . . Atlas! He's got shoulders like Atlas!

MAMA (*panting*): Isn't he out yet? I don't know how much longer I can take it.

PAPA: Keep pushing, here comes his stomach. We're just past his belly and now here's the part I've waited through three daughters for, here it, here it—

*(Silence.)*

It can't be.

*(PAPA looks at the baby closely.)*

MR. STICKY: Our Father who art in heaven . . .

LABIA: Star light, star bright, first star I see tonight . . .

HYMEN: *Nam yo ho reng ge kyo . . .*

VULVA: Hail Mary Full of Grace . . .

MR. STICKY: Hallowed be thy name, thy kingdom come . . .

LABIA: First star I see tonight I wish I may I wish I might . . .

HYMEN: *Nam yo ho reng ge kyo* . . .

VULVA: Four balls and take first base . . .

MR. STICKY: Thy will be done . . .

*(They freeze.)*

MAMA: Is he out yet, Papa? I'm getting a little woo woo—

PAPA: Push harder, Mama, maybe it's still stuck in there. If it comes out now I can attach it.

MAMA: Attach? Is my baby missing something? Is he, is he deformed?

PAPA: He's worse than deformed. He's a girl!

MAMA: A girl??!! It can't, it can't—maybe they're twins. Look inside and see if there's another one in there. There's got to be a boy hiding in there somewhere. I did everything.

*(PAPA peers into her womb.)*

PAPA (*dejectedly*): Nothing. Another girl. I'm doomed to be a child my whole life.

MAMA (*after a beat*): Dr. Papa. Stand up.

*(PAPA looks at her defeatedly.)*

MAMA: Stand up and hand me that baby.

*(PAPA stands and gives MAMA UBER ALLES the baby.)*

MAMA: Now give me something to wrap it in. Something blue.

PAPA: But blue is for—

MAMA: Just hand it to me. (*She wraps the baby in a blue blanket.*)

MAMA: Now go on and show him to everyone. They're all waiting. Show them the baby wrapped in a blue blanket. Go on. Show them what we've got.

(PAPA *takes the baby from* MAMA UBER ALLES *and walks out onto the balcony. He clears his throat.* MR. STICKY, HYMEN, VULVA, *and* LABIA *unfreeze from their positions and silently, but with great anticipation, turn towards him.*

*Haltingly,* PAPA *lifts the baby in the blue blanket up for everyone to see. They are silent for a moment, then—)*

ALL: IT'S A BOY!!!!

PAPA (*hesitantly*): It's a boy.

ALL (*congratulating each other*): IT'S A BOY!!!!

PAPA (*gaining confidence*): It's a boy.

ALL: AT LAST A BOY!!!!

PAPA (*with much pride*): AT LONG LAST A BABY BOY!!!!

ALL: WHAT'S HIS NAME?!!!

PAPA (*euphoric*): A BOY A BOY!!!!

ALL: HIS NAME IS BOY!!!!

PAPA: MY BOY MY BOY!!!!

ALL: WE'LL CALL HIM BOY!!

PAPA: Boy Uber Alles!!

ALL: BOY!!

PAPA: Uber Alles!!

ALL: BOY!!

PAPA: Uber Alles!!

ALL: BOY!!

PAPA: Uber Alles!!

ALL including PAPA: BOY!!!

# from TRUE WEST
## (Act 1, Scene 1)

BY SAM SHEPARD

**M**oral choices make for great theater. As characters wrestle between possible paths, the audience is reminded of the ethical decisions they've made in their own lives. This is a classic brothers scene by a giant of our theater.

*Characters* (appearing in this excerpt)

AUSTIN, early thirties; light blue sports shirt, light tan cardigan sweater, clean blue jeans, white tennis shoes

LEE, his older brother, early forties; filthy white T-shirt, tattered brown overcoat covered with dust, dark blue baggy suit pants from the Salvation Army, pink suede belt, pointed black forties dress shoes—scuffed up, holes in the soles—no socks, no hat, long pronounced sideburns, "Gene Vincent" hairdo, two days' growth of beard, bad teeth

*Setting*
A kitchen and adjoining alcove of an older home in a Southern California suburb, about forty miles east of Los Angeles

*Night. Sound of crickets in dark. Candlelight appears in alcove, illuminating* AUSTIN, *seated at glass table hunched over a writing notebook, pen in hand, cigarette burning in ashtray, cup of coffee, typewriter on table, stacks of paper, candle burning on table.*

*Soft moonlight fills kitchen illuminating* LEE, *beer in hand, six-pack on counter behind him. He's leaning against the sink, mildly drunk; takes a slug of beer.*

■  ■  ■

LEE: So, Mom took off for Alaska, huh?

AUSTIN: Yeah.

LEE: Sorta' left you in charge.

AUSTIN: Well, she knew I was coming down here so she offered me the place.

LEE: You keepin' the plants watered?

AUSTIN: Yeah.

LEE: Keepin' the sink clean? She don't like even a single tea leaf in the sink ya' know.

AUSTIN (*trying to concentrate on writing*): Yeah, I know.

*(Pause.)*

LEE: She gonna' be up there a long time?

AUSTIN: I don't know.

LEE: Kinda' nice for you, huh? Whole place to yourself.

AUSTIN: Yeah, it's great.

LEE: Ya' got crickets anyway. Tons a' crickets out there. (*Looks around kitchen.*) Ya' got groceries? Coffee?

AUSTIN (*looking up from writing*): What?

LEE: You got coffee?

AUSTIN: Yeah.

LEE: At's good. (*Short pause.*) Real coffee? From the bean?

AUSTIN: Yeah. You want some?

LEE: Naw. I brought some uh—(*Motions to beer.*)

AUSTIN: Help yourself to whatever's—(*Motions to refrigerator.*)

LEE: I will. Don't worry about me. I'm not the one to worry about. I mean I can uh—(*Pause.*) You always work by candlelight?

AUSTIN: No—uh—Not always.

LEE: Just sometimes?

AUSTIN (*puts pen down, rubs his eyes*): Yeah. Sometimes it's soothing.

LEE: Isn't that what the old guys did?

AUSTIN: What old guys?

LEE: The Forefathers. You know.

AUSTIN: Forefathers?

LEE: Isn't that what they did? Candlelight burning into the night? Cabins in the wilderness.

AUSTIN (*rubs hand through his hair*): I suppose.

LEE: I'm not botherin' you am I? I mean I don't wanna break into yer uh—concentration or nothin'.

AUSTIN: No, it's all right.

LEE: That's good. I mean I realize that yer line a' work demands a lota' concentration.

AUSTIN: It's okay.

LEE: You probably think that I'm not fully able to comprehend somethin' like that, huh?

AUSTIN: Like what?

LEE: That stuff yer doin'. That art. You know. Whatever you call it.

AUSTIN: It's just a little research.

LEE: You may not know it but I did a little art myself once.

AUSTIN: You did?

LEE: Yeah! I did some a' that. I fooled around with it. No future in it.

AUSTIN: What'd you do?

LEE: Never mind what I did! Just never mind about that. (*Pause.*) It was ahead of its time.

*(Pause.)*

AUSTIN: So, you went out to see the old man, huh?

LEE: Yeah, I seen him.

AUSTIN: How's he doing?

LEE: Same. He's doin' just about the same.

AUSTIN: I was down there too, you know.

LEE: What d'ya' want, an award? You want some kinda' medal? You were down there. He told me all about you.

AUSTIN: What'd he say?

LEE: He told me. Don't worry.

*(Pause.)*

AUSTIN: Well—

LEE: You don't have to say nothin'.

AUSTIN: I wasn't.

LEE: Yeah, you were gonna' make somethin' up. Somethin' brilliant.

*(Pause.)*

AUSTIN: You going to be down here very long, Lee?

LEE: Might be. Depends on a few things.

AUSTIN: You got some friends down here?

LEE (*laughs*): I know a few people. Yeah.

AUSTIN: Well, you can stay here as long as I'm here.

LEE: I don't need your permission do I?

AUSTIN: No.

LEE: I mean she's my mother too, right?

AUSTIN: Right.

LEE: She might've just as easily asked me to take care of her place as you.

AUSTIN: That's right.

LEE: I mean I know how to water plants.

*(Long pause.)*

AUSTIN: So you don't know how long you'll be staying then?

LEE: Depends mostly on houses, ya' know.

AUSTIN: Houses?

LEE: Yeah. Houses. Electric devices. Stuff like that. I gotta' make a little tour first.

*(Short pause.)*

AUSTIN: Lee, why don't you just try another neighborhood, all right?

LEE (*laughs*): What'sa' matter with this neighborhood? This is a great neighborhood. Lush. Good class a' people. Not many dogs.

AUSTIN: Well, our uh—Our mother just happens to live here. That's all.

LEE: Nobody's gonna' know. All they know is somethin's missing. That's all. She'll never even hear about it. Nobody's gonna' know.

AUSTIN: You're going to get picked up if you start walking around here at night.

LEE: Me? I'm gonna' git picked up? What about you? You stick out like a sore thumb. Look at you. You think yer regular lookin'?

AUSTIN: I've got too much to deal with here to be worrying about—

LEE: Yer not gonna' have to worry about me! I've been doin' all right without you. I haven't been anywhere near you for five years! Now isn't that true?

AUSTIN: Yeah.

LEE: So you don't have to worry about me. I'm a free agent.

AUSTIN: All right.

LEE: Now all I wanna' do is borrow yer car.

AUSTIN: No!

LEE: Just fer a day. One day.

AUSTIN: No!

LEE: I won't take it outside a twenty-mile radius. I promise ya'. You can check the speedometer.

AUSTIN: You're not borrowing my car! That's all there is to it.

*(Pause.)*

LEE: Then I'll just take the damn thing.

AUSTIN: Lee, look—I don't want any trouble, all right?

LEE: That's a dumb line. That is a dumb fuckin' line. You git paid fer dreamin' up a line like that?

AUSTIN: Look, I can give you some money if you need money.

(LEE *suddenly lunges at* AUSTIN, *grabs him violently by the shirt and shakes him with tremendous power.*)

LEE: Don't you say that to me! Don't you ever say that to me! (*Just as suddenly he turns him loose, pushes him away and backs off.*) You may be able to git away with that with the Old Man. Git him tanked up for a week! Buy him off with yer Hollywood blood money, but not me! I can git my own money my own way. Big money!

AUSTIN: I was just making an offer.

LEE: Yeah, well keep it to yourself!

(*Long pause.*)

Those are the most monotonous fuckin' crickets I ever heard in my life.

AUSTIN: I kinda' like the sound.

LEE: Yeah. Supposed to be able to tell the temperature by the number a' pulses. You believe that?

AUSTIN: The temperature?

LEE: Yeah. The air. How hot it is.

AUSTIN: How do you do that?

LEE: I don't know. Some woman told me that. She was a botanist. So I believed her.

AUSTIN: Where'd you meet her?

LEE: What?

AUSTIN: The woman botanist?

LEE: I met her on the desert. I been spendin' a lota' time on the desert.

AUSTIN: What were you doing out there?

LEE (*pause, stares in space*): I forgit. Had me a pit bull there for a while but I lost him.

AUSTIN: Pit bull?

LEE: Fightin' dog. Damn I made some good money off that little dog. Real good money.

*(Pause.)*

AUSTIN: You could come up north with me, you know.

LEE: What's up there?

AUSTIN: My family.

LEE: Oh, that's right, you got the wife and kiddies now don't ya'. The house, the car, the whole slam. That's right.

AUSTIN: You could spend a couple days. See how you like it. I've got an extra room.

LEE: Too cold up there.

*(Pause.)*

AUSTIN: You want to sleep for a while?

LEE (*pause, stares at* AUSTIN): I don't sleep.

*(Lights to black.)*

# from OUT!

BY LAWRENCE KELLY

**H**ere the playwright mixes docudrama and melodrama to create a prizewinning drama about America's favorite pastime.

In 1919, the Chicago White Sox were heavy favorites to win the World Series, but they lost to Cincinnati. Later it came out that some players had taken money to throw the Series. They became known as the "Black Sox." This excerpt begins on the field during the first game of the Series. The players discover that throwing a game is not as easy as one might think. This is a perfect example of a script as a code the reader has to crack. Within the game is another game, which is the central theme to the play.

*Characters*

EDDIE CICOTTE, star pitcher

"SHOELESS JOE" JACKSON, left fielder and heavy hitter

OSCAR "HAP" FELSCH, center fielder

CHARLES "SWEDE" RISBERG, shortstop

GEORGE "BUCK" WEAVER, third baseman

ARNOLD "CHICK" GANDIL, first baseman

CLAUDE "LEFTY" WILLIAMS, pitcher

FRED MCMULLIN, utility player

*Time*
Fall 1919

*Place*
Chicago, Illinois

*Setting*
On the field

> *As the scene opens, the players stand in a line onstage and sing the last two lines of the "Star Spangled Banner"—". . . the land of the free and the home of the brave." They break and go to their positions, ad-libbing chatter.* WILLIAMS, *who is not pitching today, is sitting off to the side with* MCMULLIN, *who is not playing.* CICOTTE *is pitching;* GANDIL, *playing first base;* RISBERG, *shortstop;* WEAVER, *third base;* JACKSON, *left field; and* FELSCH, *center field. It is Game 1 of the World Series.*

■    ■    ■

CICOTTE: I've faced Rath before. Never had any problems with him. He's not a strong hitter. Can run like a rabbit though.

*(There is baseball banter all through these scenes.)*

WILLIAMS: Come on, Eddie!
GANDIL: Go get 'em, boy!
WEAVER: Sit him down, Eddie! Sit 'em down!
CICOTTE: Maybe I better throw around him.

*(CICOTTE winds up and throws ball toward audience, which represents the hitter. After he throws the ball ALL PLAYERS just stare straight ahead. Not a word is said. After a while GANDIL walks slowly over to CICOTTE at the pitcher's mound. Long pause.)*

GANDIL: Hit him right in the head.
CICOTTE: Think he's okay?
GANDIL: Sure. He's getting up now.
WEAVER *(sarcastic)*: Nice pitch. Great way to start the World Series.
JACKSON: Loosen up, Eddie!
WEAVER: All right, get this guy!
GANDIL *(to CICOTTE)*: Take it easy. *(Goes back to first.)*
CICOTTE: Daubert has a good stick. Tough hitter. I better keep it away from him. *(CICOTTE winds up and throws.)*

*(Pause.)*

WEAVER: Four straight balls. Great. First and second, nobody out.

(GANDIL *walks to* CICOTTE.)

CICOTTE: How'm I doin'?

GANDIL: Don't make it too obvious. You can throw a strike once in a while.

WILLIAMS (*to* MCMULLIN): Cicotte's a jerk.

MCMULLIN: I think he has brain damage.

FELSCH: He keeps this up we're bound to get found out.

RISBERG: That's what I'd like to see. I hope they slaughter us.

(GANDIL *goes back to first.*)

JACKSON: Concentrate, Eddie!

WEAVER: How 'bout it, Eddie?! Big strikeout, kid!

WILLIAMS: Throw it in there, Eddie! Go get him!

CICOTTE: First and second, nobody out. Groh's up. Big hitter but I can strike him out. Maybe I better. (*Winds and throws.*)

(*Pause.*)

WEAVER: Great. Hit him right in the back.

GANDIL (*runs to mound*): Are you out of your goddam mind?

CICOTTE: It slipped out of my hand. I tried to strike him out.

GANDIL: Well, start throwing some strikes. Don't be a jerk. Don't make it so obvious.

CICOTTE: I'm trying my best.

WEAVER: Get him out of there now. He's off.

WILLIAMS (*to* McMULLIN): Bases loaded.

McMULLIN: Nobody out.

FELSCH: Come on, Eddie! Settle down!

JACKSON: This is garbage. To hell with them all. I'm playin' to win.

(CICOTTE *winds and throws. There is baseball banter all through the next section. A hit to left that* JACKSON *throws to* RISBERG, *who misses the tag.* ALL PLAYERS *react to the same action that is taking place, which the director will choreograph. Except* GANDIL, *who speaks to the audience while the banter continues behind him.*)

GANDIL: Cicotte settled down after the first inning. We had a one-one tie goin' into the fourth. I told Eddie we had to fall behind, so he just laid the ball in there for them to hit. Cincinnati smacked the hell out of him in the fourth inning. They scored five runs. Cicotte got taken out of the game.

(CICOTTE *walks to bench where he is cajoled by* WILLIAMS *and* McMULLIN.)

(GANDIL *continues*) Lefty didn't come on to pitch 'cause he was pitching tomorrow. Wilkinson pitched. Lucky for us he's not any good. We lost the game nine to one. Lefty pitched Game 2.

(WILLIAMS *walks to mound and pitches.*)

(GANDIL *continues*) In the fourth inning he gave up three walks and Kopf hit a triple for three runs. We lost Game 2, four to two. Game 3 was a total disaster. We messed up bad. Dickie Kerr was pitching for us. It just didn't go our way. We won.

# from LA BÊTE

**B**e careful when you decide to tell someone off. You may be the one who winds up looking foolish . . . In this witty, flavorful excerpt from *La Bête,* Elomire, the leader of a troupe of actors, has been ordered by his patron, the Prince, to hire the popular Valere, a man he despises, and to produce his play. Furious, Elomire tells Valere just what he thinks of him.

*Characters* (appearing in this excerpt)

ELOMIRE, leader of the troupe

BEJART, his second in command

VALERE, a troubadour

*Time*
1654

*Place*
Prince Conti's estate in Pezenas
Languedoc, France

*Setting*

The antechamber of the dining room in the actor's cottage: a blazing white environment furnished with a gilt chair and table. Busts of Greek and Roman orators line the cornice.

*Playwright's Note*

This play is meant to be performed in an absurdly high-comic style, at lightning speed and with rhymes and iambs respected. The costumes are seventeenth-century *bouffe*.

■   ■   ■

VALERE:

                                    Wait!
O, good idea! Now I can concentrate!

*(He looks ostentatiously riveted.)*

ELOMIRE:

I'm glad you're concentrating. Listen closely:
You've said a lot tonight and said it grossly.
In fact . . . I've been appalled by every word!
I find your views on life and art absurd,
And yet one hardly notices above
The mountain of your towering self-love!
Your ignorance is even more colossal—
Your brain is like some prehistoric fossil:
It must have died ten thousand years ago!
But on and on and on and on you go
As if you were the fount of human learning!
And selfishly, contemptuously spurning
The moves that others make to interject,
You act as if you're one of "the elect"
Whom God appoints like Jesus Christ our Savior!
It really is contemptible behavior
Whose only saving grace (if one there be)
Is in the unintended comedy

Arising from your weightiest pronouncements!
You seem to feel you have to make announcements
Instead of speaking in a normal tone;
But by your orotund and overblown
And hectoringly pompous presentation,
You simply magnify the desolation,
The vast aridity within your soul!
In short, I think you're just a gaping hole—
A talentless, obnoxious pile of goo!
I don't want anything to do with you!
I can't imagine anyone who would!
And if it makes me better understood
To summarize in thirty words or less,
I'd say you have the power to depress
With every single syllable you speak,
With every monologue that takes a week,
And every self-adoring witticism! . . .

VALERE:

Well, do you mean this as a *criticism?*

ELOMIRE: (*Throws up his hands; to* BEJART.)

I rest my case.

VALERE:

And when you say "depress"
Do you mean *bad* "depress" or *good* "depress"?

And overblown's defined exactly *how?*

ELOMIRE:

There, Bejart? Do you believe me *now?*

VALERE:

Would it be overreaching to request
That you write down, so that I might digest
At greater length, and also at my leisure,
The comments you just made, which I shall treasure!

BEJART:

I'm flabbergasted! I don't understand!
I've never heard a more perverse demand!
Why would you want them written down?

VALERE:

                                      To read them.

BEJART:

Well, yes. Of course. But why?

VALERE:

                              I'm going to need them.

BEJART:

But *why?*

VALERE:

Because I'm anxious to *improve!*
Is that so strange, my wanting to remove
The flaws from my persona? Surely not!
I loathe a blemish! I despise a spot!
Perfection is the goal towards which I strive
(For me, that's what it means to be alive)
And, hence, I'm grateful for a shrewd critique:
It keeps my talent honest, so to speak!
We of the theatre share that common view—
The criticisms of the things we do
Inspire our interest, not our hurt or rage:
We know it's part of "being on the stage"
To have oneself assessed at every turn,
And thus we show a willingness to learn
From judgments which might wound another man.
I much prefer to any drooling fan
A critic who will SLICE me into parts!
GOD *LOVE* THE CRITICS! *BLESS* THEIR PICKY
    HEARTS!
Precisely, and in no uncertain terms,
They halve the apple, showing us our worms.

*(Staggering slightly.)*

(My God, that was a *brilliant* illustration!)


*(Regaining himself.)*


Don't get me wrong: to hear some dissertation
On all one's failings gives a twinge of course:
It smarts when someone knocks you off your horse—
That's true for anybody I should think!
But climbing on again in half a wink
And knowing that you're better for the spill
Instructs us that it's love and not ill-will
That motivates a critical assault.
You've *honored* me tonight by finding fault!
Which doesn't mean I don't feel vaguely crushed . . .
I *do!* I'm *bruised!* But who would not have blushed
To hear himself discussed so centrally?
"My God," I thought, "Are they denouncing *me,*
These men of such *distinction* and *renown!*?
How thrilling *I'm* the one they're tearing down!!
What joy that Elomire, whom people say
Is destined to become the next Corneille,
Should slander *me* in such a public forum!"
And, by the way, it isn't just decorum
Which prompts me to express my awe of you;
Your plays, I think, show genius, and a few
(Like *Mandarin*) I've seen five times or more.
Now there's a play that really made me roar!
I haven't laughed so hard in years and years!

ELOMIRE:

It was a tragedy.

VALERE:

But through my *tears*
The laughter seemed more painful . . . (O MY GOD!
WELL, OPEN MOUTH, INSERT THY FOOT, YOU
    CLOD!
COULD THAT HAVE BEEN MORE AWKWARD?
SURELY NOT!

*(Fanning himself.)*

I'M SO EMBARRASSED! WHEW! MY FACE IS HOT!)
Forgive me, Elomire. What can I say?
I'm sure it was a very solemn play.
But why, then, did *I* find it such a hoot?
The crippled peasant boy who played the flute:
Hysterical! I mean I was delirious!
I must have nodded off when it got serious!
Are you quite sure it was a tragedy?

*(BEJART intervenes sternly, extending his hand to VALERE.)*

BEJART:

It's time to say goodnight, it seems to me.

# "SORRY"

## from *for colored girls who have considered suicide/ when the rainbow is enuf*

A CHOREOPOEM BY NTOZAKE SHANGE

"**S**orry" is one of twenty poems that make up this choreo-poem. The choreopoem, or poem with action, is one of the oldest performance forms. Here Ntozake Shange uses this direct and compelling style of play to present "the words of a young black girl growing up, her triumphs & errors, our struggle to become all that is forbidden in our environment, all that is forfeited by our gender, all that we have forgotten."

*Characters* (appearing in this excerpt)

LADY IN BLUE

LADY IN YELLOW

LADY IN BROWN

LADY IN PURPLE

LADY IN GREEN

LADY IN ORANGE

LADY IN RED

■   ■   ■

*lady in blue*
that niggah will be back tomorrow, sayin 'i'm sorry'

*lady in yellow*
get this, last week my ol man came in sayin, 'i don't
    know
how she got yr number baby, i'm sorry'

*lady in brown*
no this one is it, 'o baby, ya know i waz high, i'm sorry'

*lady in purple*
'i'm only human, and inadequacy is what makes us
    human, &
if we was perfect we wdnt have nothin to strive for,
    so you
might as well go on and forgive me pretty baby, cause
    i'm sorry'

*lady in green*
'shut up bitch, i told you i waz sorry'

*lady in orange*
no this one is it, 'i do ya like i do ya cause i thot
ya could take it, now i'm sorry'

*lady in red*
'now i know that ya know i love ya, but i aint ever gonna
love ya like ya want me to love ya, i'm sorry'

*lady in blue*
one thing i don't need
is any more apologies
i got sorry greetin me at my front door
you can keep yrs
i dont know what to do wit em
they dont open doors
or bring the sun back
they dont make me happy
or get a mornin paper
didnt nobody stop usin my tears to wash cars
cuz a sorry

i am simply tired
of collectin
     i didnt know
     i was so important toyou'
i'm gonna haveta throw some away
i cant get to the clothes in my closet
for alla the sorries
i'm gonna tack a sign to my door
leave a message by the phone
     'if you called
     to say yr sorry
     call somebody
     else

i dont use em anymore'
i let sorry/ didnt meanta/ & how cd i know abt that
take a walk down a dark & musty street in brooklyn
i'm gonna do exactly what i want to
& i wont be sorry for none of it
letta sorry soothe yr soul/ i'm gonna soothe mine

you were always inconsistent
doin somethin & then bein sorry
beatin my heart to death
talkin bout you sorry

# from BABY WITH THE BATHWATER
## (Act II, Scene 4)

BY CHRISTOPHER DURANG

T he works of Christopher Durang always put me in mind of a high wire act. His characters do their thing, have their say, perched precariously between the twin abysses of comedy and tragedy. One wrong step and they fall forever. The wonder is that they retain their balance, and complete their crossings.

In this excerpt, tragedy is pushed, pulled, shook and twisted to the point where it becomes wildly and absurdly comic.

*Characters* (appearing in this excerpt)

A YOUNG MAN

VOICE (male)

*Setting*

A blank stage, a simple white spot. From a loudspeaker at the back of the auditorium we hear a male voice—serious, sympathetic in a detached, businesslike manner.

■  ■  ■

VOICE: Come in please.

*(Enter a* YOUNG MAN *in a simple, modest dress. His haircut, shoes, and socks, though, are traditionally masculine. He looks out to the back of the auditorium to where the voice is originating from. The young man seems shy, polite, tentative.)*

State your name please.

YOUNG MAN: Daisy.

VOICE: How old are you?

DAISY: I'm seventeen.

VOICE: I wish I had gotten your case earlier. Why are you wearing a dress?

DAISY: Oh, I'm sorry, am I? *(Looks, is embarrassed.)* I didn't realize. I know I'm a boy . . . young man. It's just I was so used to wearing dresses for so long that some mornings I wake up and I just forget. *(Thoughtfully, somewhat to himself.)* I should really just clear all the dresses out of my closet.

VOICE: Why did you used to wear dresses?

DAISY: Well, that's how my parents dressed me. They said they didn't know what sex I was, but it had to be one of two, so they made a guess, and they just guessed wrong.

VOICE: Are your genitals in any way misleading?

DAISY: No, I don't believe so. I don't think my parents ever really looked. They didn't want to intrude. It was a kind of politeness on their part. My mother is sort of delicate, and my father rests a lot.

VOICE: Did you think they acted out of politeness?

DAISY: Well, probably. It all got straightened out eventually. When I was eleven, I came across this medical book that had pictures in it, and I realized I looked more like a boy than a girl, but my mother had always wanted a girl or a best-seller, and I didn't want to disappoint her. But then some days, I don't know what gets into me, I would just feel like striking out at them. So I'd wait till she was having one of her crying fits, and I took the book to her—I was twelve now—and I said, Have you ever seen this book? Are you totally insane? Why have you named me Daisy? Everyone else has always said I was a boy, what's the *matter* with you? And she kept crying and she said something about Judith Krantz and something about being out of Shake-n-Bake chicken, and then she said, I want to die; and then she said, *perhaps* you're a boy, but we don't want to jump to any hasty conclusions, so why don't we just wait, and we'd see if I menstruated or not. And I asked her what that word meant, and she slapped me and washed my mouth out with soap. Then she apologized and hugged me, and said she was a bad mother. Then she washed *her* mouth out with soap. Then she tied me to the kitchen table and turned on all the gas jets and said it would be just a little while longer for the both of us. Then my father came home and he turned off the gas jets and untied me. Then when he asked if dinner was ready, she lay on the kitchen floor and wouldn't move, and he said, I guess not, and then he sort of crouched next to the refrigerator and tried to read a book, but I don't think he was really reading, because he never turned any of the pages. And then eventually, since nothing else seemed to be happening, I just went to bed.

*(Fairly long pause.)*

VOICE: How did you feel about this?

DAISY: Well, I knew something was wrong with them. But then they meant well, and I felt that somewhere in all that, they actually cared for me—after all, she washed *her* mouth with soap too, and he untied me. And so I forgave them because they meant well. I tried to understand them. I felt sorry for them. I considered suicide.

VOICE: That's the end of the first session.

*(Lights change. In view of the audience, DAISY removes his girl's clothing and changes into men's clothing—pants and a shirt, maybe a sweater. As he changes we hear the "Hush little baby" theme played rather quickly, as on a speeded-up music box. The change should be as fast and as simple as possible. Lights come up and focus on DAISY again.)*

This is your second session. How old are you?

DAISY: I'm nineteen now.

VOICE: Why have you waited two years between your first and second sessions? And you never called to cancel them. I've been waiting here for two years.

DAISY: I'm sorry. I should have called. I was just too depressed to get here. And I'm in college now, and I've owed this paper on Jonathan Swift and *Gulliver's Travels* for one and a half *years*. I keep trying to write it, but I just have this terrible problem *beginning* it.

VOICE: In problems of this sort, it's best to begin at the beginning, follow through to the middle, and continue on until the ending.

DAISY: Ah, well, I've tried that. But I don't seem to get very far. I'm still on the first sentence. "Jonathan Swift's *Gulliver's Travels* is a biting, bitter work that . . ." I keep getting stuck on the "that."

VOICE: I see you're wearing men's clothing today.

DAISY (*with a sense of decisiveness*): I threw all my dresses away. And I'm going to change my name from Daisy. I'm considering Francis or Hillary or Marion.

VOICE: Any other names?

DAISY: Rocky.

VOICE: Have you seen your parents lately?

DAISY: I try not to. They call me and they cry and so on, but I hold the receiver away from my ear. And then I go next to the refrigerator and I crouch for several days.

VOICE: How are you doing in school?

DAISY: I'm not even sure I'm *registered*. It's not just the Jonathan Swift paper I owe. I owe a paper comparing a George Herbert poem with a Shakespeare sonnet; I owe a paper on characterization in *The Canterbury Tales;* and an essay on the American character as seen in Henry James's *Daisy Miller.* (DAISY *looks off into the distance, and sings softly.*)

> Daisy, Daisy,
> Give me your answer, do,

I'm half-crazy . . .
(*He looks grave, sad, repeats the line.*)
I'm half-crazy . . .

(*His sadness increases, he speaks slowly.*) " 'I am half-sick of shadows,' said the Lady of Shallot."

VOICE: You sound like an English major.

DAISY (*his attention returns to the* VOICE): Yes. I learned a certain love of literature from my parents. My mother is a writer. She is the author of the Cliff Notes to *Scruples* and *Princess Daisy*. And my father liked reading. When he was next to the refrigerator, he would often read. I like reading. I have this eerie dream, though, sometimes that I'm a baby in my crib and somebody is reading aloud to me from what I think is *Mommie Dearest,* and then this great big dog keeps snarling at me, and then this enormous truck or bus or something drops down from the sky, and it kills me. (*With a half-joking, half-serious disappointment that he's not dead.*) Then I always wake up.

VOICE: That's the end of our second session.

(*The lights change abruptly. From now on, these abrupt light changes—probably a center spot with side lighting that switches side to side on each change—will represent time passing and finding* DAISY *in the midst of other sessions.*)

DAISY: Doctor, I'm so depressed I can hardly talk on the phone. It's like I can only function two hours a day at maximum. I have this enormous desire to feel absolutely nothing.

VOICE: That's the end of our third session.

*(Lights change abruptly.)*

DAISY: You know, when I *do* get up, I sleep with people obsessively. I'm always checking people out on the street to see who I can sleep with.

VOICE: Eventually you'll get a lot of venereal diseases.

DAISY: I know, I already have. It's just that during the sex, there's always ten or twenty seconds during which I forget *who I am* and *where I am.* And that's why I'm so obsessive. But it's ridiculous to spend hours and hours seeking sex just really in order to find those ten or twenty seconds. It's so *time consuming!* I mean, no wonder I never get that paper on *Gulliver's Travels* done.

VOICE: Oh, you still haven't done that paper?

DAISY: No. I've been a freshman for five years now. I'm never going to graduate. At registration every fall, people just laugh at me.

VOICE: That's the end of our fifty-third session. See you Tuesday.

*(Lights change.)*

DAISY *(incensed)*: I mean it's the *inconsistency* I hate them most for! One minute they're cooing and cuddling and feeding me NyQuil, and the next minute they're turning on the gas jets, or lying on the floor, or threatening to step on my back. How *dare* they treat me like that? What's the matter with them! I didn't ask to be brought into the world. If they didn't know how to raise a child, they should have gotten a dog; or a kitten—they're more independent—or a *gerbil!* But left me *unborn.*

VOICE: That's the end of our two hundred and fifteenth session.

*(Lights change.)*

DAISY: I passed this couple on the street yesterday, and they had this four-year-old walking between them, and the two parents were fighting and you could just *tell* that they were insane. And I wanted to snatch that child from them and . . .

VOICE: And what?

DAISY: I don't know. Hurl it in front of a car, I guess. It was too late to save it. But at least it would be dead.

VOICE: That's the end of our three hundred and seventy-seventh session.

*(Lights change.)*

DAISY (*worn out by years of talking*): Look, I suppose my parents aren't actually evil, and maybe my plan of hiring a hit person to kill them is going too far. They're not evil, they're just disturbed. And they mean well. *But meaning well is not enough.*

VOICE: How's your *Gulliver's Travels* paper going?

DAISY: I'm too depressed.

VOICE: I'm afraid I'm going to be on vacation next week.

DAISY (*unwilling to discuss this*): I'm not happy with my present name.

VOICE: I'll just be gone a week.

DAISY: I wore a dress last week.

VOICE: I won't be gone that long.

DAISY: And I slept with thirty people.

VOICE: I hope you enjoyed it.

DAISY: And I can't be responsible for what I might do next week.

VOICE: Please, *please,* I need a vacation.

DAISY: All right, all right, take your stupid vacation. I just hope it rains.

VOICE: You're trying to manipulate me.

DAISY: Yes, but I mean well.

*(Lights change. Very dark, a very pessimistic anger.)*

Doctor, I've been in therapy with you for *ten* years now. I have been a college freshman for six years, and a college sophomore for four years. The National Defense loan I have taken to pay for this idiotic education will take me a *lifetime* to repay. (*His voice sounds lost.*) I don't know. I just feel sort of, well, stuck.

VOICE: Yes?

DAISY: Oh. And I had another memory I'd forgotten, something else my parents did to me. It was during that period I stayed in the laundry pile.

VOICE (*his voice betraying a tiny touch of having had enough*): Yes?

DAISY: My mother had promised me I could have ice cream if I would just stand up for ten minutes and not lie in the laundry, and then when I did stand up for ten minutes, it turned out she had forgotten she was defrosting the refrigerator and the ice cream was all melted. (*Sighs.*) I mean, it was so typical of her. (*Suddenly starts to get heated up.*) She had a college education. *Who could forget they were defrosting the refrigerator???* I mean, don't you just hate her?

VOICE: How old are you?

DAISY: Twenty-seven.

VOICE: Don't you think it's about time you let go of all this?

DAISY: What?

VOICE: Don't you think you should move on with your life? Yes, your parents were impossible, but that's already happened. It's time to move on. Why don't you do your damn *Gulliver's Travels* paper? Why don't you decide on a name? My secretary has writer's cramp from changing your records from Rocky to Butch to Cain to Abel to Tootsie to Raincloud to Elizabeth the First to Elizabeth the Second to PONCHITTA PEARCE TO MARY BAKER EDDY! I mean, we know you had a rough start, but PULL YOURSELF TOGETHER! You're smart, you have resources, you can't blame them forever. MOVE ON WITH IT!

(DAISY *has listened to the above embarrassed and uncomfortable, not certain how to respond.*)

DAISY: FUCK YOU!

(*Blackout.*)

# from MA RAINEY'S BLACK BOTTOM

BY AUGUST WILSON

**O**ne of the most moving and powerful scenes in the whole of our stage literature.

*Characters* (appearing in this excerpt)

CUTLER, mid-fifties, plays guitar and trombone, leader of the group

SLOW DRAG, mid-fifties, bass player, deceptively intelligent, though he appears to be slow

LEVEE, early thirties, plays the trumpet, often gets his skill and talent confused with each other

TOLEDO, mid-fifties, piano player, the only one of the group who can read

All of the men are dressed in a style befitting the members of a successful band of the era.

*Time*
Chicago, 1927

*Setting*

The "band room" is in the basement of the recording studio building. There are benches and chairs scattered about, a piano, a row of lockers, and miscellaneous paraphernalia stacked in the corner and long-since forgotten. A mirror hangs on a wall with various posters.

■    ■    ■

CUTLER: The white man don't care nothing about Ma. The colored folks made Ma a star. White folks don't care nothing about who she is . . . what kind of music she make.

SLOW DRAG: That's the truth about that. You let her go down to one of them white-folks hotels and see how big she is.

CUTLER: Hell, she ain't got to do that. She can't even get a cab up here in the North. I'm gonna tell you something. Reverend Gates . . . you know Reverend Gates? . . . Slow Drag know who I'm talking about. Reverend Gates . . . now, I'm gonna show you how this go where the white man don't care a thing about who you is. Reverend Gates was coming from Tallahassee to Atlanta, going to see his sister, who was sick at that time with the consumption. The train come up through Thomasville, then past Moultrie, and stopped in this little town called Sigsbee . . .

LEVEE: You can stop telling that right there! That train don't stop in Sigsbee. I know what train you talking about. That train got four stops before it reach Macon to go on to Atlanta. One in Thomasville, one in Moultrie, one in Cordele . . . and it stop in Centerville.

CUTLER: Nigger, I know what I'm talking about. You gonna tell me where the train stop?

LEVEE: Hell, yeah, if you talking about it stop in Sigsbee. I'm gonna tell you the truth.

CUTLER: I'm talking about *this* train! I don't know what train you been riding. I'm talking about *this* train!

LEVEE: Ain't but one train. Ain't but one train come out of Tallahassee heading north to Atlanta, and it don't stop at Sigsbee. Tell him, Toledo . . . that train don't stop at Sigsbee. The only train that stops at Sigsbee is the Yazoo Delta, and you have to transfer at Moultrie to get it!

CUTLER: Well, hell, maybe that what he done! I don't know. I'm just telling you the man got off the train at Sigsbee . . .

LEVEE: All right . . . you telling it. Tell it your way. Just make up anything.

SLOW DRAG: Levee, leave the man alone and let him finish.

CUTLER: I ain't paying Levee no never mind.

LEVEE: Go on and tell it your way.

CUTLER: Anyway . . . Reverend Gates got off this train in Sigsbee. The train done stopped there and he figured he'd get off and check the schedule to be sure he arrive in time for somebody to pick him up. All right. While he's there checking the schedule, it come upon him that he had to go to the bathroom. Now, they ain't had no colored rest rooms at the station. The only colored rest room is an outhouse they got sitting way back two hundred yards or so from the station. All right. He in the outhouse and the train go off and leave him there. He don't know nothing about this town. Ain't never been there before—in fact, ain't never even heard of it before.

LEVEE: I heard of it! I know just where it's at . . . and he ain't got off no train coming out of Tallahassee in Sigsbee!

CUTLER: The man standing there, trying to figure out what he's gonna do . . . where this train done left him in this strange town. It started getting dark. He see where the sun's getting low in the sky and he's trying to figure out what he's gonna do, when he noticed a couple of white fellows standing across the street from this station. Just standing there, watching him. And then two or three more come up and joined the other ones. He look around, ain't seen no colored folks nowhere. He didn't know what was getting in these here fellows' minds, so he commence to walking. He ain't knowed where he was going. He just walking down the railroad tracks when he hear them call him: "Hey, nigger!" See, just like that. "Hey, nigger!" He kept on walking. They called him some more and he just keep walking. Just going down the tracks. And then he heard a gunshot where some-body done fired a gun in the air. He stopped then, you know.

TOLEDO: You don't even have to tell me no more. I know the facts of it. I done heard the same story a hundred times. It happened to me too. Same thing.

CUTLER: Naw, I'm gonna show you how the white folks don't care nothing about who or what you is. They crowded around him. These gang of mens made a circle around him. Now, he's standing there, you understand . . . got his cross around his neck like them preachers wear. Had his little Bible with him what he carry all the time. So they crowd on around him and one of them ask who he is. He told them he was Reverend Gates and that he was going to see his sister who was sick and the train left without him. And they said, "Yeah, nigger . . . but can you dance?" He looked at them and commenced to dancing. One of them reached up and tore his cross off his neck. Said he was committing a heresy by dancing with a cross and Bible. Took his Bible and tore it up and had him dancing till they got tired of watching him.

SLOW DRAG: White folks ain't never had no respect for the colored minister.

CUTLER: That's the only way he got out of there alive . . . was to dance. Ain't even had no respect for a man of God! Wanna make him into a clown. Reverend Gates sat right in my house and told me that story from his own mouth. So . . . the white folks don't care nothing about Ma Rainey. She's just another nigger who they can use to make some money.

LEVEE: What I wants to know is . . . if he's a man of God, then where the hell was God when all of this was going on? Why wasn't God looking out for him? Why didn't God strike down them crackers with some of this lightning you talk about to me?

CUTLER: Levee, you gonna burn in hell.

LEVEE: What I care about burning in hell? You talk like a fool . . . burning in hell. Why didn't God strike some of them crackers down? Tell me that! That's the question! Don't come telling me this burning-in-hell shit! He a man of God . . . why din't God strike some of them crackers down? I'll tell you why! I'll tell you the truth! It's sitting out there as plain as day! 'Cause he a white man's God. That's why! God ain't never listened to no nigger's prayers. God take a nigger's prayers and throw them in the garbage. God don't pay niggers no mind. In fact . . . God hate niggers! Hate them with all the fury in his heart. Jesus don't love you, nigger! Jesus hate your black ass! Come talking that shit to me. Talking about burning in hell! God can kiss my ass.

(CUTLER *can stand no more. He jumps up and punches* LEVEE *in the mouth. The force of the blow knocks* LEVEE *down and* CUTLER *jumps on him.*)

CUTLER: You worthless . . . That's my God! That's my God! That's my God! You wanna blaspheme my God!

(TOLEDO *and* SLOW DRAG *grab* CUTLER *and try to pull him off* LEVEE.)

SLOW DRAG: Come on, Cutler . . . let it go! It don't mean nothing!

CUTLER (*has* LEVEE *down on the floor and pounds on him with a fury*): Wanna blaspheme my God! You worthless . . . talking about my God!

(TOLEDO *and* SLOW DRAG *succeed in pulling* CUTLER *off* LEVEE, *who is bleeding at the nose and mouth.*)

LEVEE: Naw, let him go! Let him go! (*He pulls out a knife.*) That's your God, huh? That's your God, huh? Is that right? Your God, huh? All right. I'm gonna give your God a chance. I'm gonna give your God a chance. I'm gonna give him a chance to save your black ass.

*(*LEVEE *circles* CUTLER *with the knife.* CUTLER *picks up a chair to protect himself.)*

TOLEDO: Come on, Levee . . . put the knife up!

LEVEE: Stay out of this, Toledo!

TOLEDO: That ain't no way to solve nothing.

*(*LEVEE *alternately swipes at* CUTLER *during the following.)*

LEVEE: I'm calling Cutler's God! I'm talking to Cutler's God! You hear me? Cutler's God! I'm calling Cutler's God. Come on and save this nigger! Strike me down before I cut his throat!

SLOW DRAG: Watch him, Cutler! Put that knife up, Levee!

LEVEE *(to* CUTLER*)*: I'm calling your God! I'm gonna give him a chance to save you! I'm calling your God! We gonna find out whose God he is!

CUTLER: You gonna burn in hell, nigger!

LEVEE: Cutler's God! Come on and save this nigger! Come on and save him like you did my mama! Save him like you did my mama! I heard her when she called you! I heard her when she said, "Lord, have mercy! Jesus, help me! Please, God, have mercy on me, Lord Jesus, help me!" And did you turn your back? Did you turn your back, mother-fucker? Did you turn your back? *(*LEVEE *becomes so caught up in his dialogue with God that he forgets about* CUTLER *and begins to stab upward in the air, trying to reach God.)* Come on! Come on and turn your back on me! Turn your back on me! Come on! Where is you? Come on and turn your back on me! Turn your back on me, motherfucker! I'll cut your heart out! Come on, turn your back on me! Come on! What's the matter? Where is you? Come on and turn your back on me! Come on, what you scared of? Turn your back on me! Come on! Coward, motherfucker! (LEVEE *folds his knife and stands triumphantly.*) Your God ain't shit, Cutler.

*(The lights fade to black.)*

# Biographical Notes

GARY BONASORTE is the author of *Reinventing Daddy.* Other recent plays include *The Aunts* (produced off-Broadway), *Killing Real Estate Women, Ascendency, The Marie Antoinette Society* (finalist in Steppenwolf Theatre "New Plays Project," produced in the Source Theatre Company's 1994 Washington Theatre Festival); *The Constitution Play* (commissioned by Wolf Trap in celebration of the two hundredth anniversary of the United States Constitution), and *Virginia Woolf—The Early Years* (awarded the Phi Beta Kappa award for creative achievement at Bucknell University). Mr. Bonasorte is currently director of special events at the Dramatists Guild in New York City; he is cofounder of a research clinic (CRIA) for HIV disease in New York City.

CYNTHIA L. COOPER's *How She Played the Game,* produced Off-Broadway by the Woman's Project and by Primary Stages as well as at dozens of venues in the U.S. and Canada, is included in *Women Heroes, More Golden Apples, Great Monologues* and *Baseball Monologues.* Other plays include a musical for young people about Louis Braille (Theatreworks USA), *Sisters of Sisters* (Hutchinson Festival winner), *Fox and Hounds* (Double Image Festival winner), *Slow Burn,* and *Reachin',* all performed off-Broadway in New York. A two-time Jerome Fellow at the Playwrights' Center in Minneapolis, she lives in New York City and is the author of several nonfiction books, including *Mockery of Justice: The True Story of the Sheppard Murder Case.*

CHRISTOPHER DURANG won an Obie for *Sister Mary Ignatius Explains It All for You,* a Tony nomination for *A History of the Amer-*

*ican Film,* and a Drama Desk Award for his performance in *Das Lusitania Songspiel.* His most recent play, *Sex and Longing,* opened on Broadway in 1996.

WILLIAM FINN won Tony Awards for Best Score and Best Book for *Falsettos* in 1992. He has also received the Outer Critics Circle Award for Best Musical and two Los Angeles Drama Critics Awards.

RICHARD FOREMAN founded the Ontological-Hysteric Theater in 1968. Since then he has written, designed, and directed thirty original works staged in the United States and throughout Europe. He has also written, designed, and directed eleven productions of seven musical works created in collaboration with composer Stanley Silverman. In addition, he has designed and directed works by Brecht, Buchner, Mozart, Molière, Gertrude Stein, Botho Strauss, Philip Glass, Kathy Acker, and Vaclav Havel.

SEAN HARTLEY, composer/lyricist/playwright/performer/director/teacher, is currently director of the Theater Wing at the Elaine Kaufman Cultural Center and artistic director of the Poppy Seed Players, for whom he has written several musical plays, including *A Tree Grows Up* and *Young Moses.* Sean is the primary songwriter for the award-winning musical revue *Paranoise,* in which he also appears. Publications include: *Judy and the Maccabees* (a Hanukkah tale for children) and several magazine articles.

DAVID HIRSON is the author of *La Bête,* which won the John Gassner Award of the Outer Critics Circle, the New York Newsday/Oppenheimer Award, the Marton Prize of the Dramatists Guild, the special Best Play citation in *Best Plays 1990–91,* as well as nominations for five Tony Awards and six Drama Desk Awards, including Best Play 1991. In London, *La Bête* won the Laurence Olivier Award for Comedy of the Year.

ED HOWARD, coauthor and director of *Greater Tuna* and its sequel, *A Tuna Christmas;* also coauthored the *Greater Tuna* teleplay that aired on HBO. He has directed *Greater Tuna* at the Hartford Stage Company, Houston's Alley Theatre, Circle in the Square, and the Kennedy Center in Washington, D.C., as well as on many national tours. In 1979 he cofounded the Production Company of Atlanta and Austin with Jaston Williams.

DAVID HENRY HWANG is the author of *FOB* (1981 Obie Award, Best New Play; Drama-Logue Award), *The Dance and the Railroad* (Drama Desk nomination, *CINE* Golden Eagle Award), *Family Devotions* (Drama Desk nomination), *The House of Sleeping Beauties,* and *The Sound of a Voice* (Drama-Logue Award), all of which were produced at the New York Shakespeare Festival. *Rich Relations* premiered in 1986 at The Second Stage, and *1000 Airplanes on the Roof,* a collaboration with Philip Glass and designer Jerome Sirlin toured North America, Europe and Australia in 1988–89. *M. Butterfly* opened on Broadway in 1988 and was honored with the Tony, Drama Desk, Outer Critics Circle, and John Gassner Awards. Mr. Hwang is a recipient of Guggenheim, Rockefeller, NEA, and NYSCA Fellowships. Mr. Hwang was born in 1957 of Chinese immigrant parents; he received his undergraduate degree from Stanford University in 1979 and also attended the Yale School of Drama.

DAVID IVES was born in Chicago and educated at Northwestern University and the Yale School of Drama where he was the first recipient of the Audrey Wood Scholarship in Playwriting. His plays have been performed in New York, Los Angeles, Chicago, Minneapolis, Cambridge, and at the Williamstown Theatre Festival, where he was Playwright-in-Residence in 1983. Other titles include: *Sure Thing, The Universal Language, Philip Glass Buys a Loaf of Bread, The Philadelphia,* and *Variations on the Death of Trotsky.*

LAWRENCE KELLY is an actor, teacher, and playwright. His play *OUT!* opened off-Broadway in 1985, winning much critical acclaim and a Drama Desk Award nomination. *OUT!* subsequently saw productions in Washington, D.C., Philadelphia, and Berkeley. Kelly is a graduate of the American Academy of Dramatic Arts (which he attended on a Catholic Actors Guild Scholarship), holds a master's degree from Dowling College, and teaches English and drama in NYC. He lives on the Upper West Side of Manhattan with his wife and two daughters.

JAMES LAPINE collaborated with Stephen Sondheim on *Sunday in the Park with George,* for which he was cowinner of the Pulitzer Prize, and *Into the Woods.* With William Finn, Lapine received the 1992 Tony Award for Best Book for *Falsettos.*

JOHN A. LEGUIZAMO won the 1991 Obie and Outer Critics Circle Awards for his first one-man show, *Mambo Mouth,* and in 1992 the Lucille Lortel Award for Best Actor in an Off-Broadway Play for *Spic-O-Rama,* which won the Dramatists Guild's Hull-Warriner Award for Best Play of 1992. Both have been broadcast on HBO, and the film version of *Mambo Mouth* received four ACE nominations. John was raised in Jackson Heights, Queens, and studied drama at New York University.

KATE ROTHSCHILD is the writer/director of the sketch comedy troupe Fasten Your Seatbelts. She has written, directed and performed throughout New York City, at Chicago City Limits, NADA, the Westbeth Theatre, and the Kraine Theatre. Kate received her B.A. from Brown University, where she majored in international relations.

JOE SEARS, coauthor of the hit Off-Broadway comedies *Greater Tuna* and *A Tuna Christmas,* was born and raised on the Great Plains and most of his writing reflects those influences. He received the Los Angeles Drama-Logue Award for his writing and performance in *Greater Tuna,* and in 1993, the Los Angeles Drama-Logue Award for Best Actor for *A Tuna Christmas.*

NTOZAKE SHANGE (pronounced En-toe-ZAK-kay SHONG-gay) is a playwright, poet, and novelist. In 1976 *for colored girls who have considered suicide/when the rainbow is enuf* debuted on Broadway. An Obie winner and a critically acclaimed PBS production, it was soon followed by *Spell #7, A Photograph: Lovers in Motion,* and *Boogie-Woogie Landscapes.* Ntozake Shange is also the author of several volumes of poetry and criticism.

SAM SHEPARD has written forty-five plays; eleven have won Obies. In 1979 he was awarded the Pulitzer Prize for Drama for his play *Buried Child.* He has appeared in sixteen films. In 1984 he received an Oscar nomination for his performance in *The Right Stuff.* His screenplay for *Paris, Texas* won the Golden Palm Award at the 1984 Cannes Film Festival. In 1988 he wrote and directed *Far North. Curse of the Starving Class, True West, Fool for Love, A Lie of the Mind,* and *Simpatico* are among his best-known plays. In 1986 he was elected to the American Academy of Arts and Letters. He received a Gold Medal for Drama from the Academy. In 1994 he was inducted into the Theatre Hall of Fame.

ANNA DEAVERE SMITH, an actress, playwright, and performance artist, is an associate professor of drama at Stanford University. *Fires in the Mirror* was awarded a Special Citation Obie and was runner-up for the 1992 Pulitzer Prize for drama. Ms. Smith is the recipient of numerous theater honors and awards, including a Drama-Logue Award and a Drama Desk Award.

DIANA SON lives in New York City. *Boy* premiered at La Jolla Playhouse under the direction of Michael Greif in June 1996. *Fishes* was commissioned by the Public Theatre and was performed in the Mark Taper Forum's Festival of New Works in 1995. *R.A.W.* (*'Cause I'm a Woman*) is featured in the anthology *Contemporary Plays by Women of Color.* Other productions include: *Stealing Fire* (Soho Rep); *R.A.W.* (*'Cause I'm a Woman*) (The Public Theatre, Theatre Mu, Smith College, New WORLD Theatre, and HERE); *The Joyless Bad Luck Club* (HERE); and *2000 MILES* (Ensemble Studio Theatre and Synchronicity Space).

JASTON WILLIAMS, a native Texan, acted and coauthored *Greater Tuna* and its sequel, *A Tuna Christmas.* He is the recipient of the Texas Governor's Award for his contribution to the arts. He received the Los Angeles Drama-Logue Award for ensemble acting for *A Tuna Christmas* and for acting and writing in *Greater Tuna.* In 1979 he cofounded the Production Company of Atlanta and Austin with Ed Howard.

AUGUST WILSON is a major American playwright. *Ma Rainey's Black Bottom* won the New York Drama Critics Circle Award for Best Play 1984–85. *Fences* won numerous awards for best play of 1987, including the Tony, New York Drama Critics Circle, and Drama Desk Awards, and the Pulitzer Prize. *Joe Turner's Come and Gone* was named best play for 1987–88 by the New York Drama Critics Circle. *The Piano Lesson* won the 1990 Pulitzer Prize for Drama. *Seven Guitars* opened on Broadway in 1996.

GEORGE C. WOLFE is the author of *The Colored Museum* and *Spunk,* adapted from three tales by Zora Neale Hurston. He was the director of *Angels in America* on Broadway and is the producer of the New York Shakespeare Festival.

*Permission for the use of the following
is gratefully acknowledged:*

*Hit-the-Nerve.* Copyright © 1993 by Kate Rothschild. Used by permission of the author.

"Git on Board" from *The Colored Museum.* Copyright © 1985, 1987, 1988 by George C. Wolfe. Used by permission of Grove/Atlantic, Inc.

"Are You In or Are You Out?" Copyright © 1995 by Sean Hartley; from *Paranoise.* Reprinted by permission of the author. All inquiries concerning rights should be addressed to the author, c/o the Theater Wing, Elaine Kaufman Cultural Center, 129 West 67th Street, New York, NY 10023-5967.

"Hair Anonymous Girl Look in the Mirror" from *Fires in the Mirror* by Anna Deavere Smith. Copyright © 1993 by Anna Deavere Smith. Used by permission of Doubleday, a division of Bantam Doubleday Dell Publishing Group, Inc.

"Symphony of Rats" from *Unbalancing Acts* by Richard Foreman. Copyright © 1992 by Richard Foreman. Reprinted by permission of Pantheon Books, a division of Random House, Inc.

*Greater Tuna.* Copyright © 1981, 1983 by Jaston Williams, Joe Sears, and Ed Howard. All rights reserved. CAUTION: Professionals and amateurs are hereby warned that *Greater Tuna* is subject to a royalty. It is fully protected under the copyright laws of the United States of America, and of all countries covered by the international Copyright Union (including the Dominion of Canada and the rest of the British Commonwealth) and all the countries covered by the Pan-American Copyright Convention and the Universal Copyright Convention, and of all the countries with which the United States has reciprocal copyright relations. All rights, including professional, amateur, motion picture, recitation, lecturing, public reading, radio broadcasting, television, video, or sound recording, all other forms of mechanical or electronic reproduction, such as information storage retrieval systems and photocopying, and the rights of translation into foreign languages, are strictly reserved. Particular emphasis is laid upon the matter of readings, permission for which must be secured from the Author's agent in writing. Inquiries concerning rights should be addressed to William Morris Agency, Inc., 1325 Avenue of the Americas, New York, NY 10019, Attn: Peter Franklin.

*FOB.* Copyright © 1979 by David Henry Hwang. Stage performance rights are controlled exclusively by the Dramatists Play Service, Inc., 440 Park Avenue South, New York, NY 10016. Inquiries concerning all other rights should be addressed to William Craver, Writers & Artists Agency, 19 West 44th Street, New York, NY 10036.

"Equity" from *Reachin'.* Copyright © 1987 by Cynthia L. Cooper. Reprinted by permission of the author. Originally produced by The Woman's Theatre Project, St. Paul, Minnesota. All inquiries concerning rights should be addressed to C. Cooper, 359 West 52nd Street, New York, NY 10019.

"Words, Words, Words" from *All in the Timing.* Copyright © 1994 by David Ives. Reprinted by permission of Vintage Books, a division of Random House, Inc.

*Falsettoland.* Copyright © 1989 by William Finn; from *Falsettos—Three Plays* by William Finn and James Lapine. Used by permission of Dutton Signet, a division of Penguin Books USA, Inc.

*Reinventing Daddy.* Copyright © 1994 by Gary Bonasorte. Reprinted by permission of the author. All inquiries concerning rights should be addressed to the author at 29 East 9th Street, #15, New York, NY 10003.

*Spic-O-Rama.* Copyright © 1992 by John A. Leguizamo. Used by permission of Bantam Books, a division of Bantam Doubleday Dell Publishing Group, Inc.

*Boy.* Copyright © 1994, 1996 by Diana Son. Reprinted by permission of the author's agent, Sarah Jane Leigh, International Creative Management, Inc., 40 West 57th Street, New York, NY 10019. All inquiries concerning rights should be addressed to author's agent.

*True West.* Copyright © 1981 by Sam Shepard. From *Seven Plays* by Sam Shepard. Used by permission of Bantam Books, a division of Bantam Doubleday Dell Publishing Group, Inc.

*OUT!* Copyright © 1985 by Lawrence Kelly, used by permission of the author. Inquiries concerning all rights should be addressed to the author at 175 West 92nd Street, #1H, New York, NY 10025.

*La Bête.* Copyright © 1991 by David Hirson. Reprinted by permission of the author's representative. All inquiries regarding stock and amateur rights should be addressed to Dramatists Play Service, Inc., 440 Park Avenue South, New York, NY 10016; all other inquiries should be addressed to the author's representative: Michael S. Gendler, Esq., Gendler, Codikow & Carroll, 9113 Sunset Boulevard, Los Angeles, CA 90069.

"sorry" from *for colored girls who have considered suicide/when the rainbow is enuf*. Copyright © 1975, 1976, 1977 by Ntozake Shange. Reprinted with the permission of Simon & Schuster.

Act II, Scene 4 from *Baby with the Bathwater*. Copyright © 1984 by Christopher Durang. The stock and amateur production rights to *Baby with the Bathwater* are controlled exclusively by the Dramatists Play Service, Inc., 440 Park Avenue South, New York, NY 10016. No stock or amateur performance of the play may be given without obtaining in advance the written permission of the Dramatists Play Service, Inc., and paying the requisite fee. All inquiries concerning rights (other than stock and amateur rights) should be addressed to Helen Merrill, 435 West 23rd Street, Suite 1A, New York, NY 10011.

*Ma Rainey's Black Bottom*. Copyright © 1981, 1985 by August Wilson. CAUTION: Professionals and amateurs are hereby warned that *Ma Rainey's Black Bottom*, being fully protected under the copyright laws of the United States of America, the British Commonwealth countries, including Canada, and the other countries of the Copyright Union, is subject to a royalty. All rights, including professional, amateur, motion picture, recitation, public reading, radio, television and cable broadcasting, and the rights of translation into foreign langues, are strictly reserved. Any inquiry regarding the availability of performance rights, or the purchase of individual copies of the authorized acting edition, must be directed to Samuel French, Inc., 45 West 25th Street, New York, NY 10010, with other locations in Hollywood and Toronto, Canada.

# Index

## About the Editor

Stephen Vincent Brennan, a New York actor and director, also teaches theater at the Lucy Moses School for Music and Dance. His many plays for young adults include *The Fearsome Inn, Lakota Courtship, Sundjata!,* and the acclaimed kids' *Orpheus.*

A former circus clown, Brennan now lives with his wife, Jennifer Lyons, and daughter, Lara, in Manhattan.